Business Economics

COL🔸 ᴊᴀɴᴅᴘɪʟ 🔸 Y 🔸
CA🔸
🔸

Alan Griffiths
Anglia Polytechnic University

and

Stephen Ison
Loughborough University

Series Editor
Susan Grant
Abingdon and Witney College

Heinemann Educational Publishers
Halley Court, Jordan Hill, Oxford OX2 8EJ
a division of Reed Educational & Professional Publishing Ltd

OXFORD   MELBOURNE   AUCKLAND
JOHANNESBURG   BLANTYRE   GABORONE
IBADAN   PORTSMOUTH (NH) USA   CHICAGO

Heinemann is a registered trademark of Reed Educational
& Professional Publishing Ltd

British Library Cataloguing in Publication Data
A catalogue record for this book is available from the British Library

ISBN 0 435 33221 X

Typeset and illustrated by TechType
Printed and bound by Biddles Ltd

Acknowledgements
The publishers would like to thank the following for permission to reproduce copyright material:

Addison Wesley for the table on p.56, originally appearing in Griffiths and Wall, *Applied Economics*, 2001, and the article on p72 also from Griffiths and Wall, 2000; the Advertising Association for press release no.11, October 1999; AQA for the questions on pp.29–30, 79–82, 121 (AQA examination questions are reproduced by permission of the Assessment and Qualification Alliance); BBC news website www.news.bbc.co.uk for the article dated 2 October 2000 on p.44; Causeway Press for the article on p.29 adapted from 'The Motor Industry: an economic overview' by Garel Rhys, *Development Economics*, vol.15, edited by GBJ Atkinson, Causeway Press, 1999, Ormskirk; the Congress of the United States, Congressional Budget Office for the table on p.14 which appeared in *Pricing Options for the Space Shuttle*, a CBO Special Study in March 1985; © The Economist Newspaper Ltd, London, for the articles on pp.8, 36, 86; the European Commission for the table on p.50; Edexcel Foundation for the questions on pp.88–9, 102; The *Guardian* for articles on pp.18, 19, 100; HMSO for the article and table on pp.80–1 from the *First Report on Vehicle Pricing on the House of Commons Select Committee on Trade and Industry* © Crown Copyright HMSO; The Independent Syndication for articles on pp.21, 45; *Marketing* for the table on p.77 adapted from that appearing in *Marketing* 15 March 2001; the Newspaper Society (www.newspapersoc.org.uk) for the table on p.63; OCR for questions on pp.12–14, 28, 39–41, 52–4, 102, 103–5 (reproduced with the kind permission of OCR); Office of Fair Trading (OFT) for the excerpt on p. 87 and the press release on p.98, full text available on website www.oft.gov.uk; OUP/Clarendon Press for the table on p.61 from Davies and Lyons, *Industrial Organisation in the EU*, 1996; The Telegraph Group for articles on pp.30, 40; York Publishing Services for the article on p.27 of the *British Economy Survey*, vol.29, no.2, spring 2000.

The publishers have made every effort to contact copyright holders. However, if any material has been incorrectly acknowledged, the publishers would be pleased to correct this at the earliest opportunity.

Tel: 01865 888058   www.heinemann.co.uk

Contents

Preface

Alan Griffiths and Stephen Ison are well known for their perceptive and stimulating contributions to the journal *British Economy Survey* and for the popular economic books they write.

In this new book in the series the authors explore costs and revenue of firms, the influence of market structure on firms' behaviour, and the objectives of firms and competition policy.

The key strength of the book is that is tackles these issues in both a clear way and in a real-world context, with many examples drawn from the business world.

Susan Grant
Series Editor

Introduction

The aim of the book is to combine microeconomic theory with real-world applications. This combination of theory and practice forms the basis of any study of business economics since it helps to provide a deeper understanding of the environment in which firms operate.

Chapter 1 sets out the tools and techniques of microeconomics required in order to analyse how a firm operates. It deals with production, costs and revenue, as well as providing an introduction to the concepts of the short run and the long run. Since a major objective of most firms is to maximize profits, an understanding of cost and revenue is all-important. This chapter forms the theoretical basis of the whole book because the concepts introduced here are utilized throughout the following chapters.

Chapter 2 deals with the nature and working of the markets within which firms operate. For example, it investigates why and how firms grow in size over time from both an internal and external perspective. Chapter 1 dealt with the concept of profit maximization, but firms may wish to maximize other objectives such as sales revenue, managerial utility and growth. These and other objectives are covered in Chapter 2.

Chapter 3 deals with the competitive market structure. This is a market which comprises a large number of small firms and in which resources are allocated in the most efficient manner. This market often acts as a measure against which other market structures are compared.

Chapter 4 deals with the monopoly situation in which a single firm or a group of firms (a complex monopoly) produce a significant share of the output of a given good or service. This chapter investigates the reasons for the existence of monopolies, and discusses the arguments for and against such a concentration of power.

Chapter 5 investigates a monopolistic market structure which includes elements of both perfect competition and monopoly. In particular, it analyses the nature of competition in a market where firms produce goods or services which are slightly differentiated from their competitors. As a result, this market structure involves a study of product differentiation and the role of advertising.

Chapter 6 outlines the oligopolistic market structure, where a few firms dominate the market. The chapter discusses the importance of strategic considerations in oligopoly markets and outlines the non-collusive and collusive nature of such markets.

Chapter 7 deals with contestable markets – only recently developed as a type of market structure. A contestable market is said to be similar to the competitive model outlined in Chapter 3 but with less restrictive assumptions. As a result, it can often explain real-world situations more effectively than can the model of perfect competition.

Chapter 8 deals with the nature of pricing in a practical context. It provides an insight into the different ways in which entrepreneurs decide on the price they charge for goods or services.

Chapter 9 explains how governments attempt to prevent firms from abusing their powerful position. Government influence on the business environment through competition and other types of regulatory policies is discussed.

Throughout the book, every effort is made to explain relevant economic theory in a clear and concise way. In addition, each chapter incorporates practical case study material from newspapers and reports in order to illustrate the relevance of the economic theory to the real world of business. Care has been taken to ensure that the book is as user-friendly as possible and we hope that you find it a useful introduction to business economics.

Websites

Links to appropriate websites are given throughout the book. Although these were up to date at the time of writing, it is essential for teachers to preview these sites before using them with students. This will ensure that the web address (URL) is still accurate and the content is suitable for your needs. We suggest that you bookmark useful sites and consider enabling students to access them through the school intranet. We are bringing this to your attention as we are aware of legitimate sites being appropriated illegally by people wanting to distribute unsuitable or offensive material. We strongly advise you to purchase suitable screening software so that students are protected from unsuitable sites and their material. If you do find that the links given no longer work, or the content is unsuitable, please let us know. Details of changes will be posted on our website.

Chapter One

Firms and how they operate

'Suppose one of you wants to build a tower. Will he not first sit down and estimate the cost to see if he has enough money to complete it?
Luke 14, verse 28

Production

In order to produce goods or provide services, firms require inputs of labour and capital. Labour is the *human resource*, the manual work undertaken and the mental skill required, whereas capital is a resource such as plant, machinery or factory buildings.

Capital is likely to be *fixed* in the short run – in other words it cannot be changed because new investment is usually required. Additional units of labour, however, can normally be employed in the short run, and as such can be seen as a *variable factor*.

As a firm increases its output in the short run it will experience what is known as the **law of diminishing returns**, whereby eventually the additional output declines as extra workers are employed. This can be explained by the use of Table 1 and Figure 1, but first the terms total, average and marginal product need to be defined.

- **Total product** refers to the total output that a firm produces over a period of time, with a fixed amount of capital and variable amounts of labour. Thus as the number of workers increases from none to one to two and so on, total product might increase from 0 to 40 to 100 etc.

- **Average product** refers to output per worker. It is obtained by dividing total product by the number of workers employed. So for example, if three workers are employed the average product is 70 – that is 210 divided by 3.

- **Marginal product** is the extra output obtained by employing one extra worker. Thus as seen in Table 1, if the number of workers employed is increased from two to three the change in total product, and hence the marginal product, is 110 (210–100).

The average and marginal data given in Table 1 can be reproduced in diagrammatic form as in Figure 1.

Table 1 Total, average and marginal product

Number of workers	Total product (TP)	Average product (AP)	Marginal product (MP)
0	0		
			40
1	40	40	
			60
2	100	50	
			110
3	210	70	
			50
4	260	65	
			−10
5	250	50	

In terms of the law of diminishing returns, Figure 1 illustrates that as more labour is employed then the average and marginal product will eventually decline. In this case diminishing marginal returns occurs after the second worker is employed.

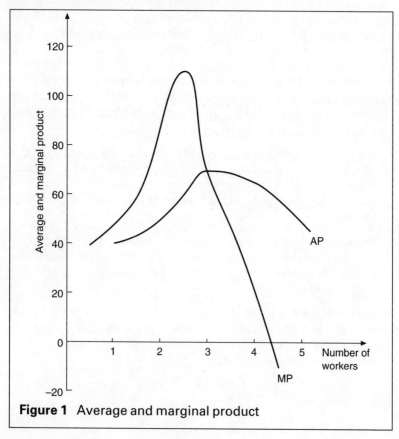

Figure 1 Average and marginal product

Costs

As well as considering product, costs need to be taken into account. In the short run certain costs will remain fixed. These **fixed costs** will have to be paid even if there is no output being produced, and include such items as the rent paid on the premises and the interest paid on loans. Certain other costs will vary as output increases. Called **variable costs**, these include items such as raw material and fuel. Table 2 gives hypothetical figures for a firm's fixed and variable costs.

In Table 2 it is possible to distinguish between total, average and marginal cost.

- **Total cost** refers to the overall cost of producing a particular amount of a particular good or level of service. This total cost can be split into fixed and variable elements, and as seen in Table 2, total fixed cost doesn't vary as output varies, being constant at £20.

- **Average cost** is the cost per unit, obtained by dividing total cost by the number of units produced (a). As with total cost it can be split into average fixed (b) and average variable (c) elements:

$$(a)\ \frac{TC}{n} \qquad (b)\ \frac{TFC}{n} \qquad (c)\ \frac{TVC}{n}$$

- **Marginal cost** refers to the change in total cost which occurs when output is changed by one unit. As such, marginal cost is: ΔTC divided by ΔQ (Greek delta stands for 'change in').

The data in Table 2 are illustrated diagrammatically in Figure 2. As can be seen, the average fixed cost declines continuously as output

Table 2 Fixed and variable costs

Output (n)	Total fixed cost (TFC) (£)	Total variable cost (TVC) (£)	Total cost (TC) (£)	Average fixed cost (AFC) (£)	Average variable cost (AVC) (£)	Average total cost (ATC) (£)	Marginal cost (MC) (£)
0	20	0	20				25
1	20	25	45	20	25	45	10
2	20	35	55	10	17.5	27.5	5
3	20	40	60	6.66	13.33	20	30
4	20	70	90	5	17.5	22.5	40
5	20	110	130	4	22	26	

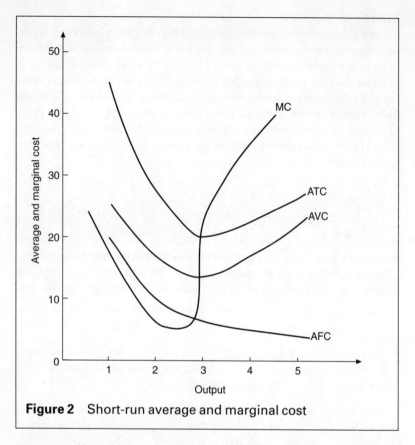

Figure 2 Short-run average and marginal cost

increases. The average variable and average total cost are U-shaped, with the vertical distance between the two curves representing the average fixed cost. The marginal cost curve is also U-shaped and it is important to note that the MC cuts the AVC and ATC curves at their minimum points.

The reason for the U-shaped average and marginal cost curves is the law of diminishing returns. Thus, if the cost of each unit of labour employed is the same, then if the marginal product is increasing the cost of each unit produced should be falling. Equally, if the firm is experiencing diminishing marginal returns the marginal product is falling and the marginal cost should therefore be rising. This is also the case with average returns and average cost, with falling average cost being the mirror image of increasing average returns. When diminishing average returns set in, the average cost begins to rise.

Long-run and short-run costs

In the long run all the inputs can be varied, which means that the firm can operate at different levels of capacity – in other words, varying the amount of capital it employs.

Figure 3 illustrates the **long-run average cost** (LRAC) curve. It is the envelope of all the **short-run average cost** (SRAC) curves and represents the lowest cost of producing a particular level of output.

The SRAC curves show how costs change with output, with capital fixed at particular levels. The SRAC curves are U-shaped because of the law of diminishing returns (see the previous section).

On the other hand, the LRAC curve is U-shaped because of **returns to scale** – or, in other words, the benefits or disbenefits of size. Up to Q^* the LRAC curve is declining, indicating that the firm is benefiting from **economies of scale**, or *increasing returns to scale* (see Chapter 2). Q^* represents the lowest point on the LRAC curve and can be referred to as the **minimum efficient scale** of production. At output above Q^* the LRAC curve increases, which signifies **diseconomies of scale**, or *decreasing returns to scale*.

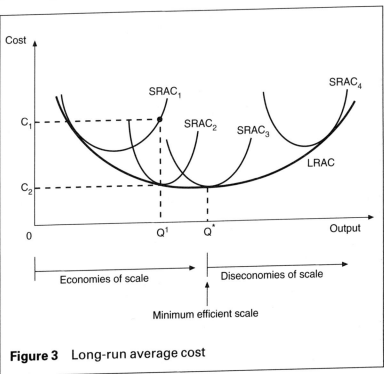

Figure 3 Long-run average cost

Knowledge is power

... an increasing number of information products ... such as software, books, movies, financial services and websites, have 'increasing returns'. Information is expensive to produce, but cheap to reproduce. High fixed costs and negligible variable costs give these industries vast potential economies of scale. A new software program might cost millions of dollars to develop, but each extra copy costs next to nothing to make, especially if it is distributed over the Internet . . . Today, if a software firm is twice as big as its competitor, its average unit costs might be up to 50% lower. This makes it harder for new entrants to break into a market.

The Economist, 21 September 2000

An output of Q_1 could be produced by a particular size of firm with a short-run average cost curve (SRAC$_1$). This would cost the firm C_1. If the firm expanded its capacity then by taking advantage of economies of scale, its costs would fall, allowing the firm to move onto the short-run average cost curve (SRAC$_2$). It could then produce output Q_1 at a lower cost, C_2. This is the lowest cost of producing Q_1 and represents a point on the LRAC curve. The whole area of economies and diseconomies of scale will be dealt with in more detail in Chapter 2.

Revenue

Table 3 gives a revenue schedule which shows how the demand for a product changes as the price changes. This is also illustrated graphically in Figure 4. In Table 3 it is possible to distinguish between total, average and marginal revenue.

Table 3 Total, average and marginal revenue

Price/Average revenue (£)	Quantity (£)	Total revenue (£)	Marginal revenue (£)
75	0	0	
			60
60	1	60	
			30
45	2	90	
			0
30	3	90	
			−30
15	4	60	
			−60
0	5	0	

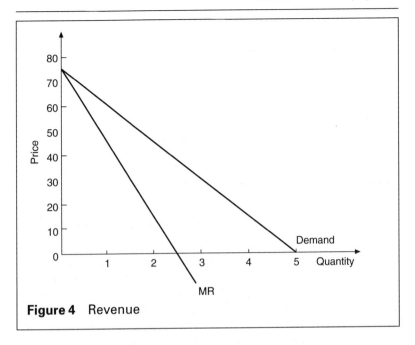

Figure 4 Revenue

- **Total revenue** refers to the price charged for the product multiplied by the quantity sold. So for example in Table 3, if the price is £15 then four units are sold and the total revenue received is £60.

- **Average revenue** is the same as the price of the product. It is obtained by dividing total revenue by quantity.

- **Marginal revenue** refers to the change in total revenue which occurs from a change of one unit in the number of goods sold. As such, marginal cost is ΔTR divided by ΔQ. So if the price falls from £60 to £45 as illustrated in Table 3, then total revenue will increase by £30, which represents the marginal revenue.

Profit maximization

The firm's profit is obtained by subtracting total cost from total revenue, thus:

$$\text{Profit} = \text{TR } minus \text{ TC}.$$

Table 4 brings together the cost and revenue figures from Tables 2 and 3. Profits are maximized where the difference between the TR and TC curves is the greatest and positive, and it can be seen that profit is maximized when an output of 2 is produced.

Table 4 Profit maximization

Output	Total Cost (£)	Marginal Cost (£)	Total Revenue (£)	Marginal Revenue (£)	Profit
0	20		0		−20
		25		60	
1	45		60		15
		10		30	
2	55		90		35
		5		0	
3	60		90		30
		30		−30	
4	90		60		−30
		40		−60	
5	130		0		−130

As before, the information given in Table 4 can be reproduced graphically (see Figure 5).

Figure 5(a) gives the situation in terms of total cost and revenue. However, as well as analysing **profit maximization** in terms of total cost and total revenue we can also view it in terms of marginal cost and revenue, as in Figure 5(b). Profit maximization is where marginal cost (MC) equals marginal revenue (MR), with MC cutting MR from below. As stated above, marginal cost represents the extra cost of producing one more unit, whereas MR is the change in revenue resulting from an increase in output by one unit. In terms of Figure 5(b) the firm will produce 2 units. Above that output, MC is greater than MR and the firm's profit will begin to fall. In Figure 5(c) it can be seen that profit is maximized at an output of 2 units.

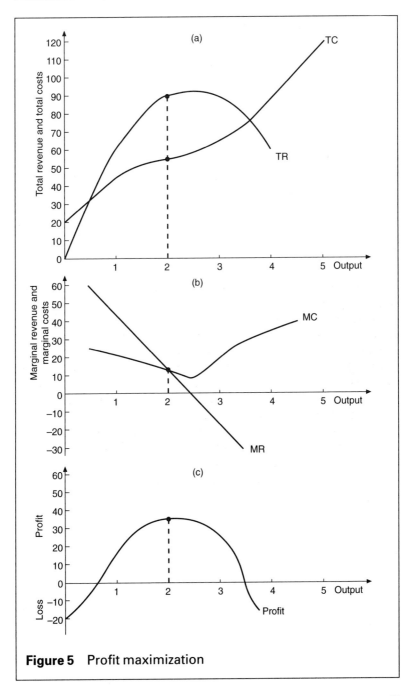

Figure 5 Profit maximization

KEY WORDS

Law of diminishing returns
Total product
Average product
Marginal product
Fixed costs
Variable costs
Total cost
Average cost
Marginal cost
Short-run costs

Long-run costs
Returns to scale
Economies of scale
Minimum efficient scale
Diseconomies of scale
Total revenue
Average revenue
Marginal revenue
Profit maximization

Further reading

Grant, S. and Vidler, C., Part 1, Units 11–13, in *Economics in Context*, Heinemann Educational, 2000.

Ison, S., Chapter 5 in *Economics*, 3rd edn, Financial Times/Prentice Hall, 2000.

Parkin, M., Powell, M. and Matthews, K., Chapters 9 and 10 in *Economics*, 3rd edn, Addison Wesley Longman, 1997.

Sloman, J., Chapter 5 in *Economics*, 4th edn, Prentice Hall Europe, 2000.

Essay topics

1. (a) Distinguish between fixed and variable costs. [10 marks]
   (b) Explain the likely effect of an increase in output on long-run marginal, average and total costs. [15 marks]
2. (a) Explain what are meant by marginal, average and total revenues. [12 marks]
   (b) Discuss at which level of output profits are maximized.
   [15 marks]

Data response question

This task is based on a question set by the former University of Cambridge Local Examinations syndicate in 1996. Read the piece below, which describes pricing options for the US Space Shuttle. Then answer the questions that follow. Your answers do not necessarily have to be limited to the material in the case.

The Space Shuttle

The Space Shuttle has been developed in the USA by the National Aeronautics and Space Administration (NASA). Its function is to put satellites into orbit for scientific, commercial and military purposes. It is not widely known that in carrying out this work, NASA applies market principles in order to determine the prices it should charge to its customers, both from the USA and elsewhere.

NASA operates in a competitive market. Its main competitors are Arianespace, operated by the European Space Agency, and a small number of private US firms. NASA estimates that, at a charge of $87m per flight, there would be an estimated demand of 24 flights per year for its services, with the competitors supplying the remainder of the market.

In determining prices, NASA has to take into account the prices charged by its main competitors who use traditional rockets which burn up in space. In contrast, the originality of the Space Shuttle is that it consists of an orbiter, which returns to earth and to which customers' rockets are attached. NASA operates four orbiters in its fleet and these can supply up to 25 flights in a year. The addition of a fifth orbiter would increase this capacity to 31 flights per year.

Table A shows the cost structure of NASA's operations. The capital charge item relates to the cost of the orbiter and the construction of the launch sites, whereas the flight costs are based on the costs incurred in putting the customers' rockets into space as required.

Economic theory advocates that resources are most efficiently used when the price which is charged is equal to the marginal cost of providing one extra unit of the particular good or service. This is the concept of allocative efficiency. In the case of the Space Shuttle, it has been estimated that the short-run marginal cost, using the four orbiters already constructed, is $42m per launch. If a further orbiter is constructed, the long-run marginal costs increase quite markedly to $75m per launch.

Table A Estimated total and average costs for the shuttle, fiscal years 1985–1990 (million $US, 1982 prices)

	1985	1986	1987	1988	1989	1990
Capital charge	1803	1760	1707	1647	1586	1529
Flight programme costs	1782	1909	1985	2021	2013	2005
Total cost	**3585**	**3669**	**3692**	**3668**	**3599**	**3534**
Number of flights	11	16	21	23	24	24
Average total cost per flight	326	229	176	159	150	147

© *Pricing Options for the Space Shuttle*, reproduced by permission of the Congress of the United States, Congressional Budget Office, 1985

1. With the aid of a diagram, explain the likely effect on the demand for the Space Shuttle of a fall in price charged by its competitors to launch the satellite. [5 marks]
2. (a) What is the difference between fixed costs and variable costs? [2 marks]
   (b) Use the information provided in Table A to allocate the costs of the Space Shuttle in terms of fixed and variable costs. Explain your answer. [3 marks]
   (c) Sketch the average total cost curve of the shuttle and comment upon its shape. [10 marks]

Chapter Two

Firm growth and objectives

'Excellent firms don't believe in excellence – only in constant improvement and constant change.'
Tom Peters

The market

Business economics is closely related to the nature and workings of the market. A market has three main features:

- It involves the exchange of goods and services, through millions of individual transactions.

- It communicates information to potential customers that goods and services – with their associated prices, qualities and quantities – are available for sale.

- It informs suppliers that there is a demand for their products.

In a pure market economy, the coordination of all this activity is done by a decentralized **price mechanism**. In such a market, the firm acts like a 'black box' which merely converts inputs into outputs to meet consumer demand at a certain price level. In other words, the firm responds to the needs of the marketplace as dictated by the price mechanism.

For markets to be perfectly efficient at allocating resources, a number of conditions need to be met. For example, the millions of transactions which take place daily in a market should occur under conditions where all those who participate in the market – both individuals and firms – have perfect knowledge of all aspects of the marketplace. In other words, a perfect marketplace would be one where information is 'costless', in that traders in different parts of the market can get in contact with each other without incurring any cost.

For example, in a perfectly efficient market there would be no need to incur the costs of advertising products, because consumers would already have 'perfect' knowledge about the products or services which the market offers. In reality, markets rarely work in such a perfectly efficient way and these imperfections are often referred to as 'market failure'. It is the failure of the market to work 'perfectly' which gives us a clue as to why firms emerge in the first place.

The emergence of firms

In reality, there are many reasons why markets are imperfect. It may be due to the fact that consumers do not have sufficient information about the choice of goods or services, so they can make rational decisions. Likewise, it may be that manufacturers mislead their customers by providing incorrect information about the quality of their products in order to increase sales. As a result of such problems, the various transactions which occur in the real marketplace often involve a high degree of uncertainty or complexity. In order to overcome some of these problems, more and more of the transactions normally done through the market are **internalised** within the company.

For example, a car manufacturer buys rubber window seals from a number of suppliers and decides how much it buys from each supplier on a short-term basis, according to the price they each tender. However, the car manufacturer may find that these suppliers become less reliable in their delivery times, or that they have used substandard materials without informing the company. Therefore the costs of such transactions (i.e. **transactions costs**) become excessive. The manufacturer might then decide that it is more efficient to set up its own internal production unit for window seals. In this way the manufacturer can consciously control the production of parts and has more control over quality, delivery times etc., rather than having to depend on the uncertainties of using external suppliers.

The advantages of *internalizing production* is a main reason for the emergence of firms. It also partially explains the rise of company mergers and acquisitions.

Over time the average size of companies in the UK has increased significantly. This has been due to factors which have influenced both the internal and external growth of firms.

Internal growth of a firm

Internal or **organic growth** can occur for a number of reasons.

Accumulation of managerial skills

Over time, managers gain a wealth of experience by working together as a team. This accumulated knowledge enables then to think of new opportunities for the firm.

Market expansion

If the market is expanding, the firms in that market sector are provided with a stimulus for growth. If they do not grow they will be left behind by other firms.

Innovation and technical change

Innovative activity and the introduction of new technology are important sources of growth for firms. They enable new products and new processes of production to be introduced that help bring down costs and create new markets. An innovative environment also stimulates further research and development which, in turn, helps firms to become even more dynamic.

Economies of scale

As the market expands, it stimulates increased production and allows a firm to reap important cost savings. In turn, as the firm becomes more cost competitive, its profit increases and it is therefore able to continue to reinvest and grow. The main **economies of scale** are those which are internal to the firm:

- *Technical economies* are savings which firms reap when they are able to take advantage of increased specialization. For example, a large firm can afford to introduce specialized machinery to help meet the market demand for the goods or service. Such specialist machinery helps lower unit costs.

- *Financial economies* are savings which can be enjoyed by large firms. For example, banks will often lend at cheaper rates of interest to such large, well-known companies, compared with the rates for smaller firms.

- *Marketing economies* are savings which larger companies enjoy as a result of being able to spread the costs of media advertising over larger levels of output – thus bringing down average advertising costs per unit sold.

- *Managerial economies* are savings which larger firms can reap because they are able to afford to employ specialists, such as accountants and salespersons, who can often increase the financial and marketing performance.

- *Commercial economies* can be enjoyed by larger firms because they can purchase supplies of raw materials or component parts in bulk and thus obtain sizeable discounts.

It is important to remember that the benefits of economies of scale noted above can be stimulated by the growth of the market which, in turn, stimulate company growth.

Big is better becomes the motto for car maker's survival

NICHOLAS BANNISTER

The motive behind the rush of motor industry takeovers and alliances in recent years has been the belief that car makers have to be big to survive.

Ford has bought Jaguar and Volvo Cars, while Daimler Benz – maker of Mercedes – has merged with Chrysler, the third largest US car manufacturer, to create a £21bn group ...

The thinking behind these mergers was that size would bring stronger purchasing power as well as economies of scale in an increasingly globalised market. Volkswagen, Europe's biggest car maker, followed this thinking when it bought Skoda and Seat, and BMW thought likewise when it bought Rover.

The cost of developing and building new models has soared as consumers have demanded more features and governments have insisted on better safety and environmental standards. The industry's response has been to concentrate on having fewer basic vehicle structures, or platforms, which can account for up to 70% of a car's cost, while offering a wider range of models on each platform.

Volkswagen, for example, offers seven different cars ranging from an upmarket Audi to a humble Skoda on just one platform. Different bodywork and interior trim create a new model at a fraction of the cost of a new platform.

The Guardian, 16 March 2000

Learning effects

The longer a firm produces a given good or service, the more experience it gains from the *cumulative* output it produces year after year. This is the **learning effect**. The experience of producing this cumulative output results in workers and managers finding better ways of producing the product or service. This, in turn, leads to a fall in costs per unit and an increase in a firm's competitiveness and its growth potential.

Diversification

Sometimes it becomes difficult for a firm to grow rapidly because the industry or sector in which it belongs is not growing fast enough. In these circumstances, a firm may find that its best strategy is **diversification** into related areas or into new products in order to grow. As a result, a firm can often benefit from **economies of scope**.

For example, savings as a result of economies of scope can be

Do It All takes over Great Mills for £285m

Nicholas Bannister

Focus Do It All (FDIA) yesterday bolstered its position as Britain's biggest independent DIY store, by agreeing to buy RMC's Great Mills retail chain for £285m.

The deal, coming only three months after FDIA's £289m acquisiton of the Wickes DIY chain, means the expanded group will have about 430 stores controlling 15% of the UK retail home improvement market ...

Economies of scale and the need for national coverage have been among the main drivers behind the recent consolidation in the DIY retail market. Stores are expanding to take in gardening, pet and crafts ranges so that the needs of the public are met under one roof ...

'The combination of FDIA, Wickes and Great Mills creates a powerful new force in the market able to compete effectively to fully exploit these opportunities,' said Bill Archer, chairman and chief executive of FDIA.

The Guardian, 7 December 2000

enjoyed when a firm lowers its unit costs as a result of producing a wide range (scope) of products that use some common component in their manufacture. Because more of the common component is made than would otherwise be the case, the overall cost per unit of this component falls, allowing the firm to become more competitive and thus aiding its growth.

In addition, the degree of diversification – and therefore the growth of the firm – depends on the nature of the market. If a firm feels that demand for a single product is rather uncertain it may prefer to produce a range of products in order to minimize the risks of having 'all its eggs in one basket'.

External growth of a firm

External growth usually takes place when two or more firms join together to form a new company. This can be done with the mutual agreement of the management of both companies (a merger), or through an attempt by one firm to acquire a controlling interest in the other firm (a takeover). There are four ways in which firms may integrate together to form a larger organization.

Horizontal integration

Horizontal integration occurs when the firms that combine together are at the same stage of production and involve similar products or services. Examples are the acquisition of Midland Bank by the Hong Kong and Shanghai Bank to form HSBC in 1992, and the acquisition of the brewing business of Whitbread plc by Interbrew, a Belgium company, in May 2000

Vertical integration

Vertical integration occurs when the firms which combine are at different stages of production of a common good or service.

Vertical backward integration refers to a situation where one firm integrates with another which is closer to the source of supply. In December 2000, for example, Centrica – the UK gas and energy supplier – acquired Avalanche Energy, a Canadian gas and oil exploration/production company, to ensure energy supplies for its distribution network.

Vertical forward integration occurs when one firm integrates with another which is nearer the market. In December 2000, for example, Imperial Tobacco bought the vending machine operations of Mayfair Vending, in order to strengthen its control over the sales of its products.

Conglomerate integration

Conglomerate integration refers to the diversification process which occurs when firms which produce different goods or services come together.

For example, between 1986 and 1995 Hanson plc acquired the Imperial Group, Consolidated Goldfields and the Eastern Group. It thus grew to become a large conglomerate in such diverse activities as tobacco, chemicals, building and energy supply. However, as the 1990s progressed many of the conglomerates such as Hanson sold off their acquisitions in order to concentrate on their core activities.

Lateral integration

Lateral integration occurs when the firms that combine provide different products but these products still have some common feature.

For example, in 1997 the Halifax's takeover of Clerical Medical – an assurance, pensions and investment company – involved the linking of different products within the same financial sector. Lloyds TSB's acquisition of Scottish Widows – a financial advice, pensions and life assurance company – in March 2000 is another example of lateral integration.

McDonald's looks back for a future

LEO LEWIS AND RAYMOND WHITAKER

Battered by the BSE and the foot and mouth crises, Ronald McDonald is going retro. Tomorrow, in the small Midwest town of Kokomo, Indiana, the company is opening the first of a planned series of resturants based on the traditional American diner ...

Lashings of chrome have been used to give the Kokomo outlet an authentic Eisenhower-era look ... If it catches on, the look may rapidly be rolled out across the McDonald's empire ...

McDonald's usual range of burgers, fries and squared-off fruit pies will be supplemented by no fewer than 122 new items, including diner classics such as meatloaf, chicken, fired steak, Belgian waffles and triple thick milk shakes ...

The venture is the latest in a series of new strategies for McDonald's which is doing its best to diversify from problem-ridden beef. Next month it is even going into the hotel business in Switzerland, opening two Golden Arch hotels near Zurich airport ... Last year McDonald's bought the Aroma chain of coffee shops, and followed that by taking a 33% stake in Prêt à Manger, clearly signalling its desire to break into the more upmarket side of the fast-food business.

The Independent, 18 March 2001

Reasons for growth through mergers and acquisitions

Valuation ratio

Mergers or acquisitions can occur when there is a difference between the value of a firm's real assets (the value of its land, buildings, machinery and equipment) and the value of the company on the stock market (the share price multiplied by the number of shares).

The ratio of market value divided by real asset value is called the **valuation ratio**. For example, a company's share price may be low on the stock exchange because its profits have fallen, while at the same time it owns valuable land in the centre of major cities. Such a combination of circumstances results in a low valuation ratio. This means, for example, that firm A can acquire firm B cheaply (because firm B's share price is low) and can therefore own valuable real assets (land in city centres) – which firm B possessed.

Market power

Mergers or acquisitions can occur when a company wants to increase its control of the market in which it operates. Such conditions can be present when international competition threatens to swamp the domestic sector, or when a fall in demand for the products of a particular industry leads to price-cutting and loss of profits. Also, government legislation to prevent firms in a particular market from colluding could lead such firms then to merge to avoid government attention.

Economies of scale/synergies

A merger or takeover usually allows the combined company to increase its scale of operations and benefit from the cost reductions explained above. Similarly, in declining industries, mergers might take place in order to eliminate any excess capacity which is present in each of the firms.

It is also possible to argue that firms may integrate in order to benefit from **synergistic factors** – the 'two plus two equals five' effect. Here, two firms may merge in order to combine complementary activities – one firm may have a strong research and development section while the other may have excellent marketing facilities.

Diversification

As well as helping to explain internal firm growth, diversification can also be important in explaining why firms merge or are acquired. One firm might acquire another because that may be the fastest way to obtain technical expertise or brands which it needs to strengthen its position in the market. Diversification can also enable one firm to enter a new industry or enable it to develop joint marketing strategies for selling similar products or services.

Managerial motivations

The intensity of merger or acquisition activity is closely related to the motives of senior managers. Such motivations are not always based on maximizing profits to the owners (shareholders), but rather are based on providing satisfaction to the managers who run the day-to-day affairs of companies. For example, managers may want to maximize the growth of the firm by merging with others, because this will provide them with greater status and power. These motivations will provide the main theme for the next part of the chapter.

Firm objectives

Profit maximization

In the long run, a major aim of a firm is to survive. To achieve this goal it has to create some measure of surplus, or profit, in order to ensure that the firm can invest for future growth.

However, it has been argued by 'neoclassical' economists that the *sole* goal of the firm is to maximize profits, and that to fulfil such a goal two conditions are necessary. Firstly, the owner of the company has to be the person who controls its day-to-day management. Secondly, the main desire of the owner has to be to achieve higher profits.

This can be seen clearly in Figure 5 on page 11, where the output for profit maximization occurs where the gap between total revenue (TR) and total cost (TC) is at a maximum, and where MR is equal to MC. In this situation, the firm is seen as a single uncomplicated organization where the ownership and control of the company is in the same hands. At the same time the firm is assumed to operate under **perfect market** conditions – i.e. to produce output as efficiently as possible in order to maximize profits.

In practice the maximization of profits is often seen as a means of maximizing *shareholder value*, because high profits help to ensure good dividends and buoyant share prices for shareholders.

However, the above assumptions of the nature of the firm are not realistic in a world dominated by large public limited companies – where the capital for such organizations is obtained by issuing shares to the general public. Two major factors make pure profit maximization very difficult to achieve in such companies.

Separation of control

First, in large corporations a separation takes place between ownership (shareholders or principals) and control (managers or agents). In other words, the owners or shareholders provide the capital, and employed managers exercise day-to-day control of the company. The main way in which the shareholders can control the managers is at the annual general meeting (AGM) of the company.

This divorce of ownership from control – sometimes referred to as the *principal–agent* problem – means that managers become relatively free from daily shareholder control and can follow their own inclinations. For example, shareholders want the firm to maximize profits so that they obtain good dividends, but managers might want to follow other goals which would give them more power and prestige.

Multiple objectives

Secondly, large corporations are no longer simple structures like the small cohesive companies described by early economists. These large organizations are complex, having many separate divisions, and it is inevitable that these divisions have different goals. For example, the production division may want to introduce a sophisticated product, but the sales division may want to sell a more simplified product which is regarded as more reliable.

Because of the complexity of the organization, it can become very difficult for the whole company to communicate effectively and, therefore, to maximize profits.

Sales revenue maximization

Economists such as William Baumol suggested that manager-controlled firms may have **sales revenue maximization** as their main goal, subject to a profit constraint – i.e. as long as profit does not fall below a critical level.

Managers are seen to want to maximize sales revenue because their salaries are often linked to the growth of sales. Likewise, the growth of sales makes it easier to attract external finance in order to expand the firm. It is also attractive to distributors and retailers because they often like products with a high turnover.

A comparison of the output of a profit maximizing firm with that of a sales-revenue maximizing firm can be seen in Figure 6. The profit is maximized at output Q_P while the sales maximizing output would be where TR is a maximum – at Q_S. Therefore a sales maximizing firm will produce more output than the profit maximizing firm and charge a lower price.

The lower price can be shown by imagining straight lines drawn from the two points X and Y to the origin (price equals total revenue TR divided by output Q). The sales maximizing price will be below the profit maximizing price because a line to Y is less steep than one to X. If the firm had to provide a minimum level of, say, π_C profit in order to pay a minimum dividend to keep shareholders happy, then the firm's output may have to be reduced to $Q_{\pi C}$.

Managerial utility maximization

This theory is associated with the name of Oliver Williamson. It revolves around the fact that since modern firms are often large, complex organizations, managers may not always have profit maximization as their key aim. Their main motivation may be to maximize their own satisfaction (utility) as long as they can produce a satisfactory profit level which keeps shareholders reasonably happy.

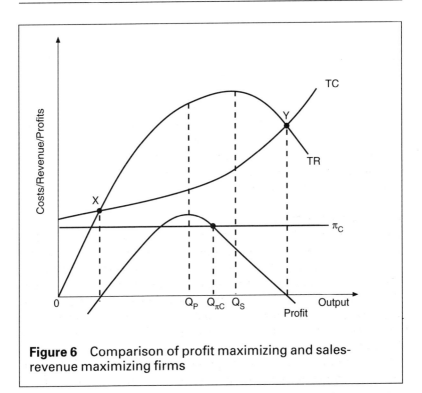

Figure 6 Comparison of profit maximizing and sales-revenue maximizing firms

For example, managers may want to maximize their own utility by awarding themselves higher salaries, and/or by employing more staff so as to increase the size of the company and therefore their own 'empire'. Similarly, managers may also keep some of the profits back in order to invest in their own pet projects – which gives them personal power and satisfaction. Managers may also obtain utility from spending on 'perks' such as company cars and lavish offices. All this provides the manager with greater power, job security and promotion prospects as the company gets larger.

However, it is worth noting that the satisfaction which managers enjoy cannot always be maximized since they still have to provide sufficient profits to keep shareholders happy.

Nevertheless, the possibility remains that managers may not be interested in maximizing profits but may sometimes incur higher costs than normal in order to satisfy their own desire for satisfaction or utility within the firm.

Growth maximization

Writers such as Robin Marris argue that the most powerful goal which managers and shareholders have in common is the *growth* of the firm. A divergence of interests between them occurs because they cannot always agree on the specific rate of growth that is desirable.

For example, shareholders may want the firm to grow so that its **share value** on the stock exchange (its capital value) increases, because this will mean that their personal wealth also grows. Managers, on the other hand, may want to see a growth in the demand for the firm's new products or services, in order to raise their status/power or salary.

When the firm makes a profit, a dilemma can arise because the shareholders might want most of the profit to be distributed to them. There is then less likelihood of the company being taken over because the company's share price will be relatively high (the company would be expensive to buy). However, as more of the profits are distributed to shareholders, less is available for managers to invest in plant and equipment to ensure the future development of new products.

If, on the other hand, too much of the profit is retained by managers and less distributed to shareholders in the form of a dividend, the share price will fall, and the company becomes relatively cheap to buy – inviting a takeover by another company.

This theory helps to show that the 'best' growth rate for a company is a balanced one, somewhere between the needs of shareholders and the needs of the managers.

Satisficing

Up to this point, the discussion about objectives of firms has been based on the maximization of certain variables, albeit under certain profit constraints. However, some writers have argued that the complexity of large organizations may make the maximization of any one goal impossible to achieve.

For example Herbert Simon argues that a firm may aim for outcomes that are acceptable or satisfactory to the main interest groups within that firm – for example, the various departments or divisions. Thus the aim here is to *satisfice,* or achieve satisfactory levels of performance which are acceptable to the main interest groups/departments.

This process is not static because a manager may set a minimum acceptable objective or satisficing level in the first instance. If that is achieved, then a new and higher objective (satisficing level) will be set next time around. If the objective is not achieved, the manager will set a lower level for the objective next time around. In this way, the satisficing levels may rise or fall over time.

This type of approach is sometimes called *behaviourist* because it concentrates on the process of decision-making within a firm rather than the managerial-type theories which tend to concentrate on the maximization of company goals.

Corporate objectives, risk taking and the market: the case of Cadbury Schweppes

ALAN GRIFFITHS

Since the spring of 1997, the business philosophy that has united Cadbury Schweppes' activities has been explained in terms of Managing for Value (MFV) ... to achieve the company's goal of increasing the value of the company to the shareholders. By 1999 the company had listed a number of objectives that it saw critical in order to meet the MFV criterion. The objectives were to:

- increase earnings per share by at least 10% every year
- generate £150m of free cash every year
- double the value of shareholder investment in the four years up to 2000
- compete in the world's growth markets by effective internal investment and by value-enhancing acquisitions
- develop market share by introducing innovations in product development, packaging and routes to market
- build strong brands that earn high margins and generate substantial cash flow
- increase commitment to value creation in managers and employers through incentive schemes and share ownership
- invest in key areas of air emissions, water, solid waste and packaging management together with soil and groundwater protection.

From the above list one can see that the first three points are clearly defined objectives that appear to follow the neoclassical preoccupation with profit ... but the fourth and fifth points stress the importance of growth and market share ... while the interesting stress on creating an environmental expenditure shows that there are many non-maximizing objectives to the company's behaviour.

Source: *British Economy Survey,* vol. 29, no. 2, spring 2000

KEY WORDS

Price mechanism
Internalized
Transactions costs
Organic growth
Economies of scale
Learning effect
Diversification
Economies of scope
Horizontal integration
Vertical integration
Conglomerate integration

Lateral integration
Valuation ratio
Synergistic factors
Perfect market
Sales revenue maximization
Managerial utility
  maximization
Growth maximization
Satisficing
Shareholder value

Further reading

Grant, S., Chapters 39 and 40 in *Stanlake's Introductory Economics*, 7th edn, Longman, 2000.

Griffiths, A. and Wall, S. (eds), Chapters 3 and 5 in *Applied Economics*, 9th edn, Financial Times/Prentice Hall, 2001.

Hornby, W., Gammie, B. and Wall, S., Chapters 4 and 5 in *Business Economics*, 2nd edn, Addison Wesley Longman, 2001.

Useful websites

Financial Times: www.ft.co.uk
National Statistics: www.statistics.gov.uk
The Guardian: www.guardian.co.uk/archive

Essay topics

1. (a) Using examples, explain the difference between internal and external economies of scale. Show how they affect the long-run average costs of a firm. [13 marks]
   (b) If there are large benefits from economies of scale, why is there so much concern about the existence of monopolies? [12 marks]
   [OCR, June 1996]
2. (a) Explain why a firm may not seek to maximize profits.

   [10 marks]
   (b) Discuss *three* other possible objectives a firm may pursue.

   [15 marks]

Data response question

This task is based on a question set by AQA in January 2001. Study the two extracts below and then answer the questions that follow. The first extract is adapted from *Developments in Economics*, vol. 15 (Causeway Press, 1999); the second extract is from the *Daily Telegraph* of 18 August 1999.

Economies of scale in the car industry

To benefit to the full from economies of scale, the most efficient car company would need to produce two million cars a year using common components. In practice, no such volumes per model are achieved anywhere in the world. Firms try to maximize economies of scale by using as many common parts as possible over a range of models. Similarly, one type of engine is used over a range of models.

Economies of scale in car manufacturing are considerable, as the following table shows. However, the table also shows that a car company increasing capacity from 100 000 to 250 000 cars a year can reduce costs at a faster rate than a much larger car company increasing its scale from 1 to 2 million cars a year.

Output of cars per year	Index of average costs per car
100 000	100
250 000	83
500 000	74
1 000 000	70
2 000 000	66

Source: Adapted from 'The motor industry: an economic overview' by Garel Rhys. *Developments in Economics*, vol. 15, edited by GBJ Atkinson, Causeway Press, 1999, Ormskirk

Sunderland car workers head productivity league

Nissan's Sunderland car plant has emerged as the most productive in Europe for the third year running, while Rover's Longbridge plant struggles at the bottom. Plants owned by the three Japanese manufacturers – Nissan, Toyota and Honda – are amongst the 10 most productive car factories in Europe, while Rover's Longbridge plant is joint 30th at the bottom of the league table. Sunderland also became Britain's biggest car plant last year, overtaking Longbridge with production up 6 per cent to 288 838.

Rover's Longbridge plant, gripped by uncertainty last year, slumped to bottom of the league table with productivity dropping almost 12 per cent and output per worker from 34 to 30. Poor sales performance may have depressed productivity.

1. Using an example from the car industry, explain the meaning of economies of scale. [5 marks]
2. Using the second extract and your economic knowledge:
   (a) Explain the meaning of labour productivity. [4 marks]
   (b) Explain possible reasons for the differences in labour productivity at Nissan's Sunderland plant *and* Rover's Longbridge plant. [6 marks]
3. In May 2000, the German car company BMW, which at that time owned Rover, sold Rover to a new owner because it could not run the British-based company profitably. Discuss the ways in which the sale of, and likely reduction in car production at, Rover cars may affect competition and prices in the UK car market. [20 marks]

Chapter Three

Competitive markets

'*By perfect competition I propose to mean a state of affairs in which the demand for the output of an individual seller is perfectly elastic.*'
Joan Robinson

Introduction

An industry or market consists of a group of firms, which produce goods or services that are close substitutes for each other. In some cases, firms in a given market produce identical products. Different markets often have different numbers of firms operating within them and this may affect the behaviour of firms in terms of the price and output decision.

This chapter deals with a market structure called a *competitive market* or **perfect competition**. This is a market in which there are a large number of firms all producing an identical product. Other market structures – monopoly, monopolistic competition, oligopoly and contestable markets – are dealt with in subsequent chapters.

A perfectly competitive market is a particular form of market structure in which resources are allocated in the most efficient manner. It is not all that common in the real world, but students of economics need to be aware of such a market since it defines the most efficient situation in terms of resource allocation.

The appeal of competition

It has long been argued by many economists that competition is a highly desirable economic state of affairs. Adam Smith in his Wealth of Nations (1776) famously argued the case in what is commonly regarded as the first economic textbook. The result of competitive forces is to produce a highly desirable state of affairs, something that cannot be matched by any alternative form of organising economies ... Perfect competition is another example of an economic model: a simplification of reality that uses assumptions to help to examine and analyse economic situations. It describes a state of affairs that represents the highest possible state of competition that could ever exist in an industry or a market.

Source: S. Munday, *Markets and Market Failure* (Heinemann Educational, 2000)

In analysing the model of perfect competition, the tools and techniques developed in Chapter 1 (namely costs and revenue) are utilized.

The model of perfect competition

The perfectly competitive market consists of many firms and can be defined as a market structure in which firms have no power over the price charged for their product. In other words they are **price-takers**, accepting the price set by the market. These markets are not likely to be found in the real world, because of the restrictive assumptions (see below), although certain markets may tend towards it. In fact, perfect competition is a market structure against which other market situations can be compared, as in Table 6 on page 57.

Assumptions for perfect competition

There are a number of assumptions made, most notably the following five.

First, there are many purchasers of the product, none of whom is significant enough to influence the market price by an individual purchase.

Secondly, there are many firms in the market. Each firm is small and not able to significantly influence the market supply by altering its own output. Therefore it cannot influence the market price of the product. Since each firm is a price-taker, its demand curve will be *perfectly elastic* at the going market price. This is illustrated in Figure 7.

In a competitive industry the price (P_0) is determined by the interaction of the market demand and supply curves, as illustrated in Figure 7(a). Since the firms are price-takers they will accept this price regardless of how much they produce. The firm's demand curve shown in Figure 7(b) is perfectly elastic – which means that an infinitely small increase in price will result in an infinitely large change in the quantity of the product demanded.

Thirdly, a key feature of a competitive market is the assumption of **perfect information**. Both firms and purchasers are aware of the price as set by the market. If one firm charges a price above the market price then purchasers, given that they have perfect information about the market, will buy the product from another firm.

Fourthly, firms operating in the market produce an identical product. In other words their is a **homogeneous product**. Therefore, purchasers are indifferent as to which firm they buy their product from. This is another reason for the demand curve being perfectly elastic as seen in Figure 7(b).

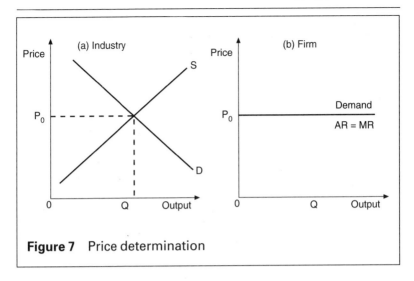

Figure 7 Price determination

Fifthly, in a competitive market there is freedom of entry into, and exit from, the industry or market. This means that firms already in the market cannot prevent new firms entering the industry, and this will have an influence on the profits earned. In fact in the long run all firms will earn **normal profit**.

Normal profit

Normal profit can be defined as the profit necessary to keep the firm operating in the long run and, as such, it can be seen as a cost of production. The cost curve includes all essential costs and the entrepreneur (as with labour) needs a certain reward (profit) to operate the business. It is an essential cost, which needs to be paid for the entrepreneur to exist and the firm to operate. In other words, unless firms can earn normal profit they will eventually leave the industry.

Short-run equilibrium in a competitive market

As stated in Chapter 1, the *short run* can be defined as a period of time in which at least one of the factors of production is fixed. This is the period of time in which new firms will be unable to enter the market. It is possible, therefore, by taking the firm's demand curve and short-run costs to determine the **short-run equilibrium** for a firm in a competitive market. This is illustrated in Figure 8. Note first that in a competitive market a profit-maximizing firm can make **supernormal profit**, or **break even**, or make a **loss** in the short run. Which situation a firm finds

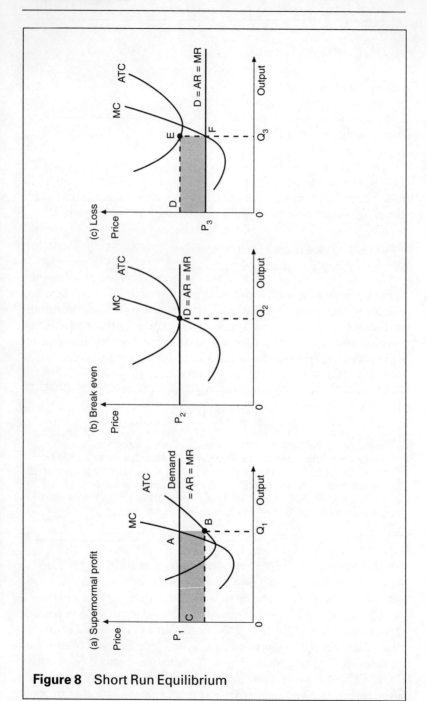

Figure 8 Short Run Equilibrium

itself in depends on whether the market price is above or below its average total cost.

In Figure 8(a) the firm is in equilibrium when marginal revenue (MR) equals marginal cost (MC), as outlined in Chapter 1. This firm is producing an output of Q_1. As stated above, the marginal and average cost curves include an element of profit, called normal profit, and since the firm is more than covering these costs the firm is making supernormal profit equal to the area P_1ABC.

In Figure 8(b) the firm is also in equilibrium, producing an output of Q_2 when MR = MC As such, it aims to maximize its profit; but unlike the firm in part (a) this firm is only just covering its average total costs and so is making normal profit. In fact the firm is said to be *breaking even*.

In Figure 8(c) the firm is producing an output of Q_3 when MR = MC. But in this situation the firm is in fact *loss-minimizing,* making a loss equal to the area P_3DEF. In such a situation the firm will close down in the long run – although it may continue to operate in the short run if it can cover its *average variable costs*. The reason for this is as follows.

In the short run a firm will continue to operate so long as it can cover its average variable (or running) costs. Even if the firm produced no output it would still have to pay the fixed costs – such items as rent for premises and the interest paid on loans the firm has taken out. If, in the short run, the firm can cover its variable costs (most notably the purchase of raw materials and its wages bill) and *some* of its fixed costs, then it is worth operating.

This is illustrated in Figure 9 with the firm producing an output of Q_0 and selling at a price of P_0. Note that fixed cost is the difference

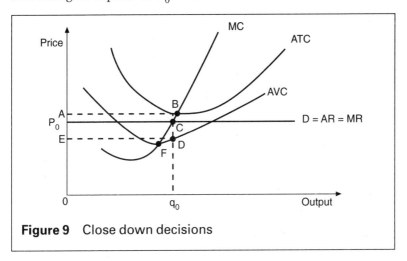

Figure 9   Close down decisions

between ATC and AVC. By operating at this output the firm is covering its total variable cost of $0EDQ_0$ and part of its total fixed cost. Its total fixed cost is given by area EABD, and by operating at output Q_0 the firm is covering EP_0CD of that cost. It is still making a loss equal to area P_0ABC, but that is less than the loss would be if the firm were *not* producing in the short run – which would be area ABDE.

Clearly if the firm continues to make a loss it will close down in the long run. Equally if price were below point F – that is, below the average variable cost – then the firm would close down even in the short run since it would not be able to cover average variable costs AVC (the purchase of raw materials and labour).

Retailing on the Internet, it is said, is almost perfectly competitive. Really?

The explosive growth of the Internet promises a new age of perfectly competitive markets. With perfect information about prices and products at their fingertips, consumers can quickly and easily find the best deals. In this brave new world, retailers' profit margins will be competed away, as they are all forced to price at cost.

Or so we are led to believe. And yes, studies do show that online retailers tend to be cheaper than conventional rivals, and that they adjust prices more finely and more often. But they also find that price dispersion (the spread between the highest and the lowest prices) is often as wide on the Internet as it is in the shopping mall – or even wider. Moreover, the retailers with the keenest prices rarely have the biggest sales.

Such price dispersion is usually a sign of market inefficiency. In an ideal competitive market, where products are identical, customers are perfectly informed, there is free market entry, a large number of buyers and sellers and no search costs, all sales are made by the retailer with the lowest price. So all prices are driven down to marginal cost. Search costs on the Internet might be expected to be lower and on-line consumers to be more easily informed about prices. So price dispersion online ought to be narrower than in conventional markets. But it does not seem to be ...

Perhaps the biggest reason for price dispersion is that consumers are willing to pay a premium to shop at sites that they trust ... even people who use 'shopbots' – computer programs that search many websites for the best deal – usually buy from the market leader even if it is not quoting the lowest price. A trusted brand may be more important on the Internet than on the high street, since online consumers pay upfront and cannot be sure whether or when their purchases will be delivered.

Adapted from *The Economist*, 18 November 1999

Long-run equilibrium in a competitive market

In the long run each firm in a competitive market will be earning normal profit and operating at the minimum point on both their short-run and long-run average cost curves, having gained all the available economies of scale. (Economies of scale were explained in Chapters 1 and 2.)

The firm in Figure 10(a) is of a size such that its short-run average and marginal cost curves are $SATC_1$ and SMC_1 respectively. With the market price of P_1 and an output of q_1 the firm is making supernormal profit equal to the shaded area. This encourages the firm to increase its capacity, allowing it to move on to a lower average and marginal cost curve such as SMC_2 and $SATC_2$ – in order to obtain economies of scale.

In addition, the existence of this supernormal profit will encourage new firms to enter the industry. This will lead to an increase in the industry supply, indicated by a shift to the right from S_1 to S_2 in Figure 10(b). Hence the market price will fall, until the long-run equilibrium price of P_2 and output of Q_2 is reached.

In terms of the individual firm illustrated in Figure 10(a), its capacity has increased such that the $SATC_2$ and SMC_2 curves are the new short-run average and marginal cost curves. The firm is now operating at the lowest point on *both* its short-run and long-run average cost curves, after obtaining the full economies of scale. The firm will be in **long-run equilibrium**, producing an output of q_2 with average costs at their minimum level at E. Any increase or decrease in output from q_2 would result in the firm making a loss.

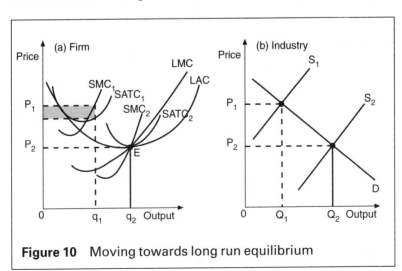

Figure 10 Moving towards long run equilibrium

Allocative and productive efficiency

If long-run equilibrium could be achieved in a perfectly competitive market, that would have important implications for the economy. For example, in business economics a fundamental issue for each firm is the optimal use of its scarce resources – and that is something achieved in a perfectly competitive market. We saw in Figure 10(a) that in the long run a perfectly competitive firm will operate where marginal cost equals the price charged – that is at E, the lowest point on the long-run average cost curve. In perfect competition consumers are charged a price which is exactly equal to what it costs the firm to produce the extra or marginal unit of output, and then **allocative efficiency** is said to occur. In other words, because price is equal to marginal cost the market is said to have achieved allocative efficiency.

Equally, since the firm is operating at the lowest point on the long-run average cost curve (so obtaining all the available economies of scale) the firm is said to be **productively efficient**. This is the case since the costs per unit of production in the long run are as low as is technically possible.

Overall, therefore, a perfectly competitive market structure produces a situation in which both allocative and productive efficiency are achieved.

KEY WORDS

Perfect competition	Supernormal profit
Price-takers	Break even
Perfect information	Loss
Homogeneous product	Long-run equilibrium
Normal profit	Allocative efficiency
Short-run equilibrium	Productive efficiency

Further reading

Bamford, C. (ed.), Chapter 3 in *Economics for AS*, Cambridge University Press, 2000.

Griffiths, A. and Wall, S., Chapter 6 in *Intermediate Microeconomics*, 2nd edn, Financial Times/Prentice Hall, 2000.

Ison, S., Chapter 6 in *Economics*, 3rd edn, Financial Times/Prentice Hall, 2000.

Munday, S., Chapters 2 and 3 in *Markets and Market Failure*, Heinemann Educational, 2000.

Essay topics

1. (a) Describe what is meant by a perfectly competitive market. [10 marks]

   (b) Explain why firms in a perfectly competitive market earn normal profits in the long run. [15 marks]

2. (a) Explain what is meant by allocative and productive efficiency. [10 marks]

   (b) Discuss whether perfectly competitive firms always achieve allocative and productive efficiency. [15 marks]

Data response question

This task is based on a question set by OCR in March 2000. Read the two pieces below, the second of which is adapted from an article in the *Daily Telegraph* of 18 August 1998. Then answer the questions that follow.

Labour market failure in London

The labour market is a good example of a market where the forces of supply and demand do not operate as expected by economic theory. A particular illustration of this market failure is in London where there are thousands of unfilled vacancies in hotels, restaurants and catering outlets. These activities invariably pay low wages, often to students and casual workers, and are typical of the employers being targeted by the government's announcement of a national minimum wage of £3.60 per hour from April 1999. Workers under 21 years old and receiving some form of training can be paid a lower rate.

Economists have analysed the effects of introducing such a minimum wage. Figure A, which assumes a perfectly competitive labour market, shows the effects of introducing a national minimum wage on low-pay occupations such as in hotels, restaurants and catering. The demand curve (D) represents the number of hours of labour that firms will wish to buy at various wage rates; the supply curve (S) shows the number of hours that workers will be willing to work at various wage rates.

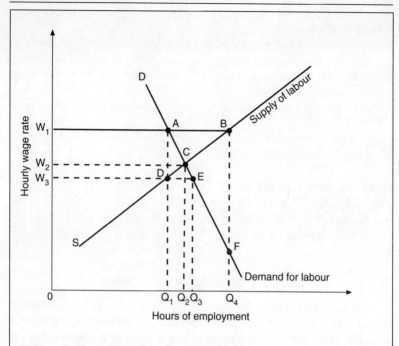

Figure A The employment effects of a minimum wage (W_1) in a perfectly competitive labour market

Joining the foreign service

London now has more restaurants per head than any other city, and the hospitality industry (as hotels, restaurants and catering outlets are now called) is the second largest employer in Britain. Many are small businesses, although, increasingly, large national and international operators account for the £2 billion spent by London's 27m tourists on food and drink.

There is a serious shortage of 'waiting staff' in London. So much so, in fact, that more and more such staff are foreign and young, despite information on vacancies not being easily accessible to prospective workers. Many employers are more than happy to employ foreign staff, not least because Britons do not like serving each other. One section of British society still willing to wait at tables though are ex-public school pupils and other students from middle-class backgrounds. They seem more prepared to work, at least temporarily, for low wages and usually have more initiative in seeking appropriate opportunities in comparison with other types of casual labour.

One restaurateur, Laurence Isaacson of Chez Gerard, thinks that it will be difficult to find the 2000 staff needed to cater for those who want to eat and drink in the Millennium Dome.

1. (a) State *four* characteristics of a 'perfectly competitive market'. [5 marks]

   (b) Use the material in the first piece to analyse the extent to which the market for 'waiting staff' in London is a perfectly competitive *labour market*. [4 marks]

2. With reference to Figure A:

   (a) At which point is the labour market in equilibrium? Explain what this means. [2 marks]

   (b) Describe the slope of the supply curve for labour and explain its significance for restaurant owners. [2 marks]

   (c) *Excluding hourly wage rates*, state and explain *two* other factors which might determine the supply of 'waiting staff' to London's restaurants. [4 marks]

3. The second piece asserts that there is a serious shortage of 'waiting staff' in London. Explain how this is represented in Figure A. [4 marks]

4. With the aid of a new diagram, explain how the wage rates of 'waiting staff' in London might be affected by the opening of the Millennium Dome. [4 marks]

Chapter Four

Monopoly

'*I don't meet competition. I crush it.*'
Charles Revson (founder of Revlon Cosmetics)

Introduction

In its purest form, a monopoly exists when a single firm produces all the output of a given good or service. Since no close substitutes exist for such products, the firm *is* the industry and the demand curve it faces is the market demand. As a result, the monopolist is a **price-maker** as compared with a perfectly competitive market where firms are **price-takers**.

In the real world, a firm can dominate an industry without needing to produce all the output of an industry. There can also be a situation – known as a **complex monopoly** – where a group of companies can get together and act as a single monopolist. For simplicity, what follows will generally refer to the single-firm monopoly, while the case study section will clarify the complex-monopoly case.

Sources of monopoly power

The main reason why monopolies exist in the economies of most countries is that they have been able to wield their power because other firms have found it difficult to enter the industry, owing to high entry barriers.

These barriers may have come about – or are strengthened – because the monopolist has enjoyed certain natural advantages over other firms, or because it has decided in a strategic way to keep such barriers high in order to maintain its monopoly position. The following are some of these barriers.

- *Increasing returns to scale.* In some industries, a firm which has a monopoly over the production of a good or service may reap economies of scale and produce near its minimum efficient scale of production (MES). However, if another competitor enters the market then each will be producing at less than its MES level. This is often called a natural monopoly situation because the size of the market is only large enough for one firm to reach the lowest cost (MES) position.

- *Ownership of key resources*. Some companies own the exclusive rights to critical raw materials, making it difficult for other firms to enter the industry to compete.

- *Patent or copyright protection*. In these circumstances a firm may have been given exclusive legal rights to use a certain invention which gives it an advantage over its competitors. Similarly firms may have an exclusive right to reproduce material such as books etc.

- *Exclusive franchise*. On some occasions, a firm has been given exclusive rights to produce or sell a good. Such rights may sometimes be granted by governments.

- *Distribution channels*. In these circumstances, the firm has acquired control over some parts of the industry's distribution network. For example, it may own/control the wholesale or retail outlets through which the product or service is sold, thus making it difficult for competitors to find suitable outlets.

- *Consumer loyalty*. A dominant firm has often built up a strong brand image over time, strengthening this by continuous advertising in order to make it difficult for new firms to enter the industry.

Behaviour and performance of monopolies

In reality, a company is unlikely to maintain its monopoly position indefinitely. Market conditions change, and some of the entry barriers noted above may disappear. Therefore the behaviour and performance of monopoly firms depends on the degree of concentration in the industry, the ease of entry and exit, and the degree to which the company has succeeded in convincing the consumer that the product or service which it sells is unique.

In terms of industry concentration, the most powerful situation would be where the firm supplies 100 per cent of the market. In practice, however, a single firm may have a dominant control over an industry if it controls as little as 25 per cent of the market – according to the criteria laid down by UK competition policy (see Chapter 8).

The ease of entry and exit depends very much on the time element, since over time it is more likely that new ways will be found to overcome barriers to entry.

Finally, in terms of product differentiation, the low *cross-elasticity of demand* (which describes a situation where a firm's product or service has little competition) is likely to change as a new generation of consumers alter the nature of demand. In the meantime we need to investigate the advantages and disadvantages of a monopoly situation.

BT under fire on fast web

MARK WARD

Industry watchdog Oftel has received a formal complaint from a group of telecoms companies over the way that high-speed net services are being introduced.

Three companies are complaining that the process of giving them access to local telephone exchanges is not being run fairly.

The trio want Oftel to take action to ensure they have the same access to exchanges that BT enjoys.

BT still controls over 80% of all the telephone lines that run from local exchanges to homes and businesses. The unbundling process is supposed to give BT's rivals access to the exchanges so they can offer consumers a better deal on high-speed net access.

Oftel has faced a barrage of criticism over the past month about the way it is handling this unbundling process.

www.news.bbc.co.uk, 2 October 2000

The argument against monopoly structures

High price and low output
A monopolist who has power over the market will produce less than the output of a competitive market and keep price above the competitive price. This will result in a welfare loss to society as a whole.

Higher costs
A monopolist may not always produce at its lowest cost since its main objective may not be cost minimization but profit maximization. Profit maximization is often achieved by producing an output level that is less than the quantity at which costs per unit are minimized. This tends to keep prices, profits and costs higher than normal.

Simply put, there is often no incentive for a monopoly to produce at the most efficient cost-reducing output because it has no immediate competitors.

Product varieties and product life cycles
It is often said that monopolists do not have an incentive to produce a variety of products which would help increase consumer choice and satisfaction. Likewise, a monopolist may keep the same model of a product for longer than would be desired by consumers.

Banks called to account for overcharging

ANDREW GARFIELD AND COLIN BROWN

The government ordered a [complex] monopoly inquiry into Britain's banks yesterday after an official investigation concluded they were overcharging every household by up to £400 a year ...

A report by the former telcoms watchdog, Don Cruickshank, accuses the banks of overcharging personal and small business clients between £3bn and £5bn a year too much ...

Mr Cruickshank had said there would be no improvement unless there was root and branch reform of the banking sector and the way it was regulated. 'My main finding is that banks have unnecessary market power that they have

been able to use over the last four to five years to make supernormal profits,' he said. High street banks are charging 'far too much' for credit cards, savings accounts and personal loans said Mr Cruickshank ...'All banks are the same' was a frequent refrain, Mr Cruickshank said.

In 1998, three UK banks made more profits than the UK's five publicly traded supermarket companies added together ... The fact that the big four – Barclays, NatWest, HSBC and Lloyds TSB – have 68% of Britain's current accounts, and 78% of all credit cards issued, highlighted the need for 'radical reform'.

The Independent, 21 March 2000

Income distribution

Monopolists often earn supernormal (i.e. above normal) profits which means that there is a shift in the distribution of income from general consumers (who pay higher prices) to companies and their shareholders.

Economic stagnation

It is argued that monopoly power leads to stagnation through a series of processes, as follows. Monopoly power leads to restrictions in output. This in turn leads to a reduction in employment. Lower employment reduces income. As a result demand falls. This causes monopoly output to decline which reduces employment / income / demand and leads to stagnation.

The argument for monopoly structures

Low price and high output

If a market is monopolized by one firm instead of a number of smaller firms, then that firm may reap the benefits of scale economies which lower costs significantly. As a result, prices fall below, and output above, the competitive level. This would lead to an increase in consumer welfare.

Lower costs

As noted above, the absolute costs under a monopoly could be lower than in the competitive market because of the possibility of scale economies. Thus, production would be at a more efficient (i.e. lower cost level) than in the competitive market.

Figure 11 compares the equilibrium situation under monopoly with that of a perfectly competitive market. We will assume for simplicity that a previously competitive industry is taken over by a monopoly with no change in cost or demand conditions.

In the initial situation, the perfectly competitive industry's supply curve is MC (obtained by summing all the individual firms' marginal cost curves, $(S = \Sigma MC_c)$. Equilibrium in this perfectly competitive market is where price $(AR) = S$; that is at point C on the diagram, with price P_C and output Q_C.

If the total market is taken over by a monopolist (so that the supply curve now becomes the monopolist's marginal cost curve, MC_{m1}), the equilibrium output of this firm (and thus of the industry) would be where $MR = MC_{m1}$; that is at output Q_M – and therefore price P_M. In other words, the monopoly price will be higher, and output lower, than the competitive market level. The monopoly position is less efficient

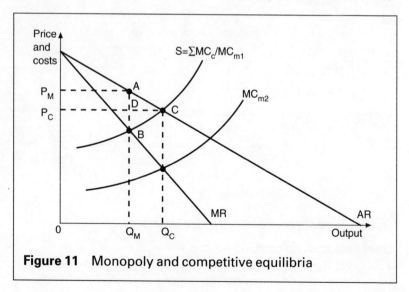

Figure 11   Monopoly and competitive equilibria

because at the output level of Q_M, price (AR) is *above* MC (by amount AB), as compared with the most efficient competitive output level Q_C, where price (AR) is *equal* to MC.

The welfare loss to consumers because of the monopolist's higher price and lower output would be equal to the area of triangle ADC. The welfare loss to producers from producing less output would be the triangle DCB. The total net loss for society would be the area ABC which is referred to as the 'deadweight loss'.

On the other hand if, as a result of intensive innovative activity, the monopolist's costs were actually *lower* than MC_{m1} – for example at MC_{m2} – then output and price could be back at their old competitive levels of P_C and Q_C once more. In this case the monopoly is as efficient as the competitive market.

Innovation

The creation of supernormal profits need not be detrimental to consumers because, whilst they allow the firm to invest in risky research which banks may not be keen to fund, this research is essential for innovation. For example, new processes of production will result in a fall in unit costs. These cost reductions would be in addition to the normal scale economies and would shift the whole average cost curve downwards.

Stability

The presence of a monopoly structure can help to maintain stability in the market. In a perfectly competitive market, there would be continuous entry and exit movements and a loss of continuity. A monopoly situation can, at least over the short run, provide stability so that skills and knowledge can be preserved during difficult economic periods. This could also help prevent the worst effects of the 'stagnation cycle' described above.

Corporate governance

Monopolies may not be a problem for society because the *threat* of takeover will keep them efficient. For example, if a monopoly firm does not produce as efficiently as it should, then its share price will fall on the stock market and it will be open to a takeover bid by another company whose managers or owners feel it can buy the company cheaply and make it more efficient.

Monopoly and price discrimination

Because the monopolist has power over the market, it may be able to increase its total profits by charging different prices for the same good or service in different markets. However, for such **price discrimination** to be successful three main conditions are required.

- *Price-maker conditions*. The firm must have sufficient power to be able to set the market price. In this situation, there is little chance of other firms entering the industry to prevent the monopolist from setting such prices.

- *Market separation conditions*. The markets must be kept separate, so that consumers in the market with the lower price cannot sell to consumers in the market with the higher price.

- *Demand conditions*. The elasticity of demand must be different in each market.

If the monopolist can set the price because of its dominant power in the market, then it can get on with the job of separating the markets and charging different prices in the different markets. This market separation can be in terms of different times of the day or night – as in the case of train or electricity charges. It can also be done geographically, such as by charging different prices for the same model of car in different countries of the EU.

Obviously, the monopolist will maximize profits by charging a lower price in the market where demand is elastic (sensitive to price changes) and a higher price in the market where demand is relatively inelastic (less sensitive to price changes).

Figure 12 shows a monopolist producer who wishes to sell an identical good or service in two separate markets in order to maximize revenue. The different prices which will be charged in the markets can be shown more clearly by using a common vertical price axis and then placing the outputs of market 1 and market 2 on each side of the price axis.

We assume that the discriminating monopolist produces a total output of $Q_1 + Q_2$ of the product or service, but has to decide how much to sell in each market in order to maximize its revenue. The demand/marginal revenues curves in markets 1and 2 are shown by D_1/MR_1 and D_2/MR_2 respectively. Finally, the common cost of producing the product or service is shown by the horizontal line, MC. The equilibrium quantity sold in each market is determined at the point where the MR curve of each market is equated to the common cost of production, MC.

Since the elasticity of demand in market 2 is greater than in market 1, then a lower price, P_2, will be charged in market 2 and a higher price,

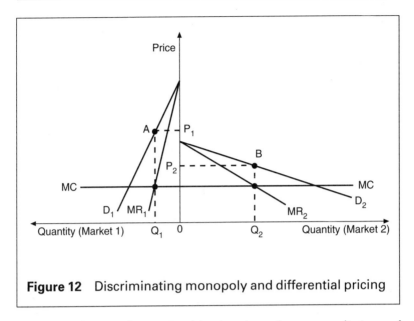

Figure 12 Discriminating monopoly and differential pricing

P_1, charged in market 1. In this situation, the monopolist's total revenue (areas $P_1AQ_10 + P_2BQ_20$) will be at its maximum level.

Monopoly case studies
In the previous sections we looked at monopoly from a theoretical perspective. This final section provides two practical case studies of monopoly behaviour.

1. UK car prices: price discrimination in a complex monopoly
In the 1990s, consumers complained that car manufacturers were charging significantly more for the same model of car in the UK than in other EU countries. Table 5 shows, for eight models, the percentage price differential between the pre-tax price in the UK and in the cheapest eurozone country in November 2000. It can be seen that prices in the UK were between 24 per cent and 90 per cent more expensive.

The Competition Commission in the UK concluded that a complex monopoly existed – whereby at least a quarter of the new cars sold in the UK were supplied by a group of manufacturers and importers who prevented or distorted competition. This was done by car manufacturers giving dealers exclusive rights to sell their cars – but only at the price, and in the locations, decided by the manufacturers.

Table 5 Car price differentials in the UK and the eurozone

Make of car	UK price difference (%)	Make of car	UK price difference (%)
Renault Laguna	90	Ford Focus	41
Fiat Bravo	67	Volkswagen Golf	41
Peugeot 306	46	Alfa Romeo 156	40
Honda Civic	42	BMW 318i	24

Source: European Commission DG COMP, November 2000

This 'exclusive dealership' situation created price discrimination on two levels:

- UK fleet cars were sold at a discount of up to 55 per cent, and this loss of revenue was recouped by selling the same model to private buyers at a higher price.

- Pre-tax prices of cars were kept at a higher level in the UK to subsidize lower pre-tax car prices in other EU countries – where the tax on cars is greater – so that consumers in those countries were not discouraged from buying the car.

To keep the markets separate, and so prevent purchases direct from cheaper EU countries, manufacturers often penalised dealers who engaged in cross-country importing by refusing to allow those dealers to sell their cars.

An in-depth analysis by the EU in November 2000 revealed that only just under a half of the difference in prices of individual car models across the countries of the EU could be explained by different taxes, dealer margins etc. in those countries. Thus, over half of the price differences seemed to be accounted for by discriminatory polices by the manufacturers.

2. Drug prices: price discrimination under a single product monopoly

In March 2001, Napp Pharmaceuticals of the UK was fined £3.2 million by the Office of Fair Trading for engaging in an abuse of its dominant power in the market for sustained-release morphine tablets. Their brand, called MST, extended the duration of action of morphine preparations, thus giving longer relief from pain to cancer sufferers.

The drug was sold to two main markets – hospitals and the community (GPs). Its market share in both markets was over 90 per cent, making it a clear monopoly producer.

The two market segments had different elasticities of demand. The community segment was relatively inelastic, because GPs in general are reluctant to experiment with new products; are strongly influenced by the reputation of a product; and are not price sensitive when considering patients with terminal pain. Also, Napp had very few competitors in this sector.

On the other hand, hospitals are generally willing to use any brand of a relatively simple compound. Purchasing decisions are coordinated across NHS regions, and purchasers look for 'good prices'. The company also faced more competitors in this market segment.

As a result, Napp gave large discounts to the hospital sector – which left the community sector paying ten times the price of the hospital sector for the same tablets. Its prices were also between 33 per cent and 67 per cent more expensive than their nearest competitors. This price discrimination was also designed to eliminate competition by engaging in **predatory pricing**, as we will see in Chapter 8.

KEY WORDS

Price-maker
Price-takers
Complex monopoly
Product life cycles

Corporate governance
Price discrimination
Predatory pricing

Further reading

Ison, S., Chapter 6 in *Economics*, 3rd edn, Financial Times/Prentice Hall, 2000.

Lipsey, R. and Chrystal, K., Chapter 10 in *Principles of Economics*, 9th edn, Oxford University Press, 1999.

Parkin, M., Powell, M. and Matthews, K., Chapter 13 in *Economics*, 4th edn, Pearson Educational, 2000.

Sloman, J., Chapters 6 and 7 in *Economics*, 4th edn, Prentice Hall Europe, 2000.

Useful websites

European Commission: www.europa.en.int/comm/dgs/annrep.htm
Office of Fair Trading: www.oft.gov.uk
The Economist: www.economist.com
The Independent: www.independent.co.uk/search

Essay topics

1. British Telecommunications (BT) is regarded by economists as a monopoly because of its dominant market share. However, in recent years other providers such as Mercury and Vodaphone have entered the market.

   (a) Explain how monopolists can earn high levels of profits.
   [10 marks]

   (b) In the summer of 1997, BT reduced the prices of many telephone calls and introduced various other discounts (e.g. Friends and Family). Discuss the likely consequences for telephone companies and telephone users.
   [15 marks]

   [UCLES, March 1999]

2. (a) Explain the sources of monopoly power.
   [10 marks]

   (b) Discuss whether a monopoly or a perfectly competitive market is more likely to benefit consumers.
   [15 marks]

Data response question

This task is based on a question set by the former University of Cambridge Local Examinations syndicate in 1996. Read the piece below, which relates to an entirely fictitious company. Then answer the questions that follow. Your answers do not necessarily have to be limited to the material in the case.

Percy Engineering Ltd

Percy Engineering is the only manufacturer in the UK of the 'Snow Pusher', a specialist type of snow-moving equipment which is attached to the front of a lorry. It was patented by its inventor and owner in 1954. The company supplies 80 per cent of all such devices used by local authorities and private contractors in the UK.

Most economists would be concerned about the behaviour of firms such as Percy Engineering which have very large shares of a particular market. It is felt that their monopoly power often allows them to restrict output, raise prices and determine their own scale of production, so enhancing company profits at the expense of the consumer. Figure A shows the overall marginal and average revenue curves (MR and AR) which the firm believes it is currently facing, along with its short-run marginal and average total cost curves (MC and ATC).

Percy Engineering has been successful in exporting Snow Pushers to the rest of the European Union, its exports reaching a peak five years ago when they accounted for about half the total revenue of the business. More recently, the company has lost some of its market share to lower-

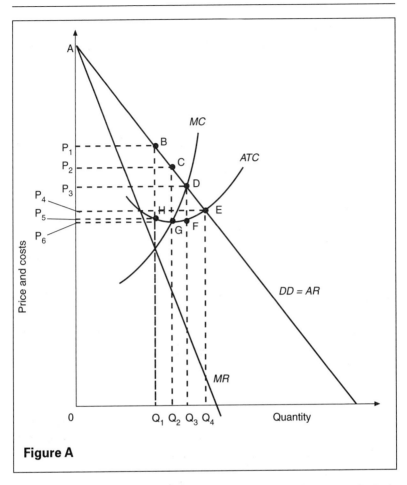

Figure A

cost producers from South East Asia, who have been particularly successful in producing a similar product for the European market.

Consequently, Percy Engineering has made losses from its business in the rest of the EU and these have had to be funded from profits earned in the UK domestic market. The firm's market share in the UK has held up well in spite of its difficulties in the rest of the EU. However, recent research by an independent group of economists has estimated that the price elasticity of demand for Snow Pushers in the UK market is less than in the rest of the EU. This has prompted Percy Engineering to review its pricing policy, which currently involves charging the same price for Snow Pushers in all of its markets.

1. (a) To what extent can Percy Engineering be considered a monopolist? [3 marks]

   (b) Describe briefly how the company originally gained its monopoly power in the UK market and how it may have subsequently retained it. [4 marks]

2. (a) Explain the term 'consumer surplus'. [2 marks]

   (b) Use Figure A to explain how consumer surplus changes if the price rises from P_2 to P_1. [4 marks]

3. (a) From Figure A, identify Percy Engineering's total level of profits at the profit-maximizing level of output if it charges the same price to all consumers. [2 marks]

   (b) Explain how the firm would not maximize profits if it produced output Q_2. [3 marks]

   (c) Explain why the firm might use price discrimination as a way of further increasing the overall profitability of its business. [6 marks]

4. Why might Percy Engineering not always maximize profits? [8 marks]

5. (a) What evidence would you collect in order to report to the government on whether Percy Engineering is currently acting against the public interest? [8 marks]

   (b) Discuss the action the government might take if the firm were found to be acting against the public interest. [10 marks]

Chapter Five

Monopolistic Competition

'The theory of monopolistic competition provides few new analytical tools; it is very similar to that of perfect competition. It furnishes a better description of those competitive industries in which product differentiation occurs – food processing, men's clothing, cotton textiles, and the service trades and health professions in large cities, for instance – in that is recognizes small monopoly elements and the consequent different prices charged by different sellers of a particular type of product.'
Richard H Leftwich and Ross D Eckert

Introduction

In the previous two chapters, we have considered two markets: one which consists of many firms which have no power over the price charged for their product, i.e. firms that are price-takers (perfect competition), and the other, where a single firm produces all of the output, i.e. a price-maker (monopoly). There are, however, many markets in which the firms are also price-makers even though there are a large number of them producing goods and services.

Price-making exists in such situations because firms produce imperfect substitutes i.e. goods and services which are slightly differentiated from their competitors An example are restaurants in any town or city. No two restaurants are the same either in the food and service they offer (Chinese, French, Greek, Indian, Italian, Mexican etc.) or where they are located. Since each restaurant is not exactly the same as its competitors then the existence of **product differentiation** means that each restaurant has some degree of monopoly power in its neighbourhood. As such, if they increase their prices they do not lose all of their customers even though they produce close substitutes to other firms in the market.

Because they are differentiated from each other, each restaurant faces a downward sloping demand curve, although it is relatively elastic. Since it is not a monopoly market, as detailed in Chapter 4, then new restaurants can enter the market because there are few barriers to entry. As such, the number of firms in the market and the conditions of entry are not too dissimilar from that of perfect competition. Since such a market combines the features from both perfect competition and

---

Product differentiation
The monopolistic element of monopolistic competition arises because the product of each firm is similar but not identical to that of other firms. Each firm therefore has some measure of monopoly power, but this is limited because the products are relatively close substitutes. Product differentiation means making goods and services slightly different from that of the firms competitors.

---

monopoly it is called *monopolistic competition*. This market is characterised by product differentiation as firms attempt, through advertising, to create their own individual brand of good or service.

Assumptions with respect to monopolistic competition
There are a number of assumptions associated with monopolistic competition:

- Firms are price makers. Since firms in this market, have an element of market power it means they are price makers and as such face a downward sloping demand curve, as in Figure 13.

- There are a large number of firms in the market each producing goods and services which are slightly different from their competitors.

Given the two assumptions above, firms believe that their actions have no effect on the price other firms can charge for their output. As such, since no one firm can affect the behaviour of other firms then:

- Firms do not act in a strategic manner. This situation is the same as for firms operating under perfect competition and monopoly, but not under oligopoly (as detailed in Chapter 6 in the section on game theory).

- There is freedom of entry into the market, which means that if there is supernormal profit to be earned, new firms will enter the market.

- Product differentiation exists.

A major difference between monopolistic competition and perfect competition is the fact that in the former the products are differentiated whereas in the latter they are identical (homogeneous). In monopolistic competition, the goods and services produced are not perfect substitutes, in other words the products are differentiated and as such the firm can increase the price of its goods or services without losing all

Table 6 Assumptions of monopolistic competition compared to perfect competition and monopoly

Assumptions	Monopolistic competition	Perfect competition	Monopoly
The firms influence on price	Firms are price makers	Firms are price takers	Firms are price makers
Number of firm in the market	Many firms. None is large relative to the overall market size	Many firms. None is large relative to the overall market size	One firm
Strategic behaviour	Since there are a large number of firms, all relatively small, there is no strategic behaviour	Since there are a large number of firms, all relatively small, there is no strategic behaviour	Since there is only one firm there is no need for strategic behaviour
Barriers to entry	Free entry into the market	Free entry into the market	High barriers of entry into the market
Substitutes between different firms goods and services	The goods and services produced are differentiated	The goods and services produced are homogeneous	There are no close substitutes

of its sales (unlike perfect competition). Therefore, each firm in monopolistic competition has an element of monopoly power, but equally, they are in a competitive situation because their products are close substitutes, like the restaurant sector mentioned earlier. The assumptions of monopolistic competition are compared with that of perfect competition and monopoly in Table 6.

Short run equilibrium in monopolistic competition

As stated, firms in monopolistic competition face a downward sloping demand curve. In the short run this is represented by D_{SR} in Figure 13. If we assume that the monopolistically competitive firm is a profit maximiser (producing where MC equals MR), it is possible

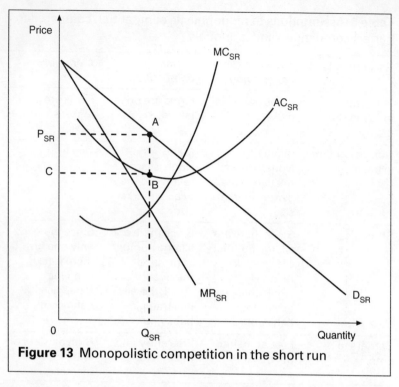

Figure 13 Monopolistic competition in the short run

for a firm to make supernormal profit in the short run. This is illustrated in Figure 13 with the firm in equilibrium producing an output of Q_{SR} and selling at a price of P_{SR}. The supernormal profit is given by the area $P_{SR}ABC$.

Figure 13 looks very similar to that of a monopolist (see page 46). The main difference is that in monopolistic competition, the figure refers to one firm rather than the whole market as under monopoly.

Long run equilibrium in monopolistic competition

Given that one of the assumptions of monopolistic competition is that there is free entry of firms into the market, then new firms will enter if there are supernormal profits to be made. As new firms enter the market, the demand curve for each individual firm in the market will shift to the left. The supernormal profit will be competed away until in the long run each firm will be earning normal profit. This is illustrated in Figure 14 when in the long run each firm is operating where D(AR) is equal to AC producing an output of Q_{LR} at a price of P_{LR}.

As can be seen in long run equilibrium, the AC curve is tangential to

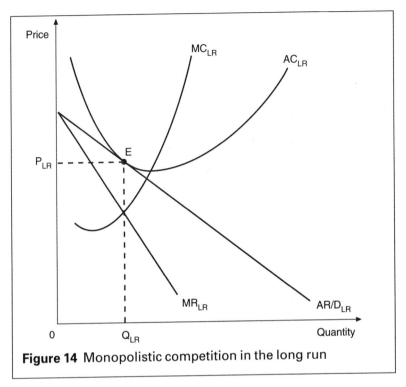

Figure 14 Monopolistic competition in the long run

the long run demand curve (D_{LR}) at E. If AC were above AR everywhere then firms would be making losses and some would ultimately leave the industry. Even though the firm is earning normal profit, in the long run it still possesses monopoly power since its demand curve is downward sloping. This is the case since the firm still experiences produce differentiation.

Monopolistic competition and efficiency

As explained in Chapter 3, perfectly competitive markets have the benefit of being efficient. The same cannot be said of monopolistically competitive markets. By comparing perfect competition and monopolistic competition in the long run, as in Figures 15(a) and (b), it can be revealed that monopolistic competition has two inefficiencies.

As can be seen in Figures 15(a) and (b), unlike perfect competition, price under monopolistic competition is greater than marginal cost (MC). In perfect competition, consumers are charged a price which is exactly equal to what it costs the firm to produce the extra of marginal unit of output (MC). Since price equals MC in the perfectly competitive

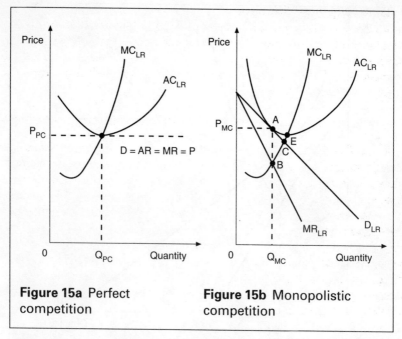

Figure 15a Perfect competition

Figure 15b Monopolistic competition

market, it is said to have achieved allocative efficiency. However, in monopolistic competition at an output of Q_{MC}, price exceeds marginal cost by AB. As such the value to the consumer exceeds the cost of producing those units. If output were expanded beyond Q_{MC} up to point C, where the demand curve crosses the MC curve, then the total surplus could be increased by area ABC. By operating at an output of Q_{MC} there is therefore a welfare loss to society (called a deadweight loss) of area ABC. This is the same problem experienced under monopoly and outlined in Chapter 4.

As seen in Figure 15(b), at an output of Q_{MC}, the firm is operating on the downward sloping portion of its average cost curve (at A). Average cost is at a minimum at point E and in monopolistic competition therefore the firm is not achieving productive efficiency. It is in fact operating with **excess capacity**. The excess capacity is an inefficiency because average cost could be lower if there were fewer firms in the market.

The marketplace and competitive strategies under monopolistic competition

As we have seen earlier, monopolistic competition tends to describe a situation in which there are a relatively large number of small or medium sized firms in the industry who sell differentiated products. In practice it is not always easy to determine which industries or product groups approach the textbook definition of monopolistic competition.

It is usually assumed that there is a large number of firms in such a marketplace. If this is so, this type of competition would most likely be found in the small and medium sized company sector who employ less than 250 employees and who accounted for around 99.9% of all UK businesses and 52% of all UK turnover in 2000.

As far as the industrial distribution of such a marketplace is concerned, it is also likely to be in markets which are not always dominated by large firms. An idea of these markets can be obtained by measuring how much of the output of a given industry is accounted for by the five largest firms (see Chapter 6 on oligopoly for more detail). Monopolistic competition would be most likely be found in an industry where a large firms do not dominate, i.e. where the five firm **concentration ratio** is low. An example of the least **concentrated industries** in the EU is given in Table 7.

As well as these industrial groups, the wholesaling and retailing trades in large urban centres would appear to operate under condition of monopolistic competition. Examples of industries and services which fit the description would be restaurants, clothes shops, opticians, shoe shops, furniture shops, computer software, paints and varnishes, costume jewellery etc. etc. However, the question remains as to how such firms manage to succeed over time.

A small or medium sized company can survive because of its *locational* attributes – i.e. it has no clear competitor in the immediate vicinity. However, a company can also survive because it has

Table 7 Selected 5-firm concentration ratios in Europe

Industry Group	Concentration ratio (5 firm)
Printing and publishing	9.3
Jewellery	8.1
Stone products	7.8
Footwear	5.8
Meat products	5.7
Plastics	5.6
Clothing	4.3
Silk	5.3
Wooden furniture	3.1

Source: Davies and Lyons (1996)

managed to *differentiate* its products from those of its rivals. This can be done in different ways. First, it can concentrate on trying to keep costs low so that it can compete more effectively on price. Second, it can offer more selection, improved quality, better credit terms, distinctive design and extra services etc. to its customers. Third, it can engage in a **specialisation strategy** where it distinguishes itself from its competitors by focusing on a limited market segment or customer group.

These differences in the potential strategies of firms in monopolistic competition arise because consumer needs and preferences are diverse. This is particularly interesting because this means that there is still room for a relatively large number of firms to compete in some industries or product segments.

This type of competition can suit consumers for two main reasons. First, firms operating under monopolistic conditions are competing in a marketplace where market forces are so dominant that buyers are relatively well protected from exploitation by sellers. Second, that the tendency for firms to engage in product differentiation often provides a stimulant to technological innovation and to expanding the range of consumer choice.

For example, research by Cambridge University Centre for Business Research in 1996 found that over 20% of small and medium sized companies in their sample produced 'original' product innovation which helped to stimulate the economy and provide more choice to the consumer.

Monopolistic competition and advertising

In a monopolistic market, one of the most powerful factors which enhances the product differentiation strategies of firms is the role of advertising. Advertising also allows consumers to *familiarise* themselves with the product or service so that consumers uncertainty is minimised.

In addition, advertising *reminds* consumers of the intrinsic value of the product or service and *spreads news* about new products that have arrived on the marketplace, thus overcoming consumer inertia. Advertising expenditure by medium and type for the year 2000 is shown in Table 8.

From Table 8 it can be seen that television is by far the most dominant medium for advertising company products and services, followed by regional newspapers, national newspapers, and magazines. Although large companies carry out much of this

Table 8 Advertising expenditure by type of medium and type (2000)

Advertising Expenditure	2000 (£m)
Television	3,949
Regional newspapers	2,762
National newspapers	2,258
Magazines	2,019
Direct mail	869
Directories	868
Posters	823
Radio	536
Internet	155
Cinema	128

Source: http://newspapersoc.org.uk/facts-figures/adspend.html

advertising, it should be remembered that many small and medium sized firms also advertise extensively. They advertise in regional newspapers, magazines and local radio which comprise a sizeable part of total advertising expenditure In this way, advertising is extremely important for these companies as a way of informing consumers of their goods and services and helping to give increased consumer choice through product differentiation.

What effect can advertising have on the prices charged for goods and services under monopolistic competition? To answer this question it is necessary to understand that advertising expenditure is an additional cost to a company and will therefore tend to shift the average cost curve (AC) upwards; while advertising, if successful, can also shift the demand curve (AR) upwards to the right. The net effect of the two shifts can be summarised in Figures 16 and 17 by using the definitions of the variables in Table 9:

Table 9

Variables	Excluding advertising	Including advertising
Demand curve	D_1	D_2
Average total cost	AC_1	AC_2
Price	P_1	P_2
Quantity	Q_1	Q_2
Equilibrium point	E_1	E_2

ADVERTISING ASSOCIATION

Advertising brings innovation, quality and consumer choice, says new study

Until 1984, the spectacles' market was highly restricted, and there was a ban on all forms of advertising other than in opticians' premises ... the ban made it difficult for new firms to enter the market and it acted as a disincentive to innovation. The removal of the blanket ban on advertising has encouraged freer competition in the market. Spending on advertising rose from £1.7m in 1985 to £10.6m in 1997. This has translated into greater choice (e.g. the introduction of designer frames); enhanced service (e.g. same day service); and lower prices (e.g. the promotion of ready-made reading glasses).

Source: Advertising Association, press release no.11, October 1999

Figures 16 and 17 illustrate just two potential equilibrium situations. To simplify the diagrams, the marginal cost/revenue curves have been omitted. In Figure 16, we can see that the combined effect of advertising on the demand and cost curves has resulted in an increase in price and a decrease in quantity of the good or service available to consumers. However in Figure 17 we see the reverse i.e. advertising has led to a fall in the price, and an increase in the quantity available to the consumers.

The price and output levels in Figures 16 and 17 depend on the particular way in which advertising changes the shape and position of the demand and cost curves. An important study of the economic effects of advertising by consultant economist Keith Boyfield in 1999 (see insert) found that advertising increases consumer choice and can bring prices down akin to the analysis shown in Figure 17. One could even argue that although advertising has led to higher price as in Figure 16, this might be worthwhile if it gives consumers a wider choice.

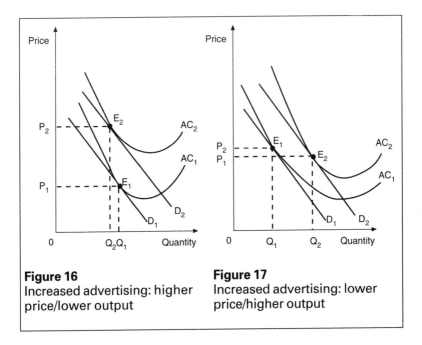

Figure 16
Increased advertising: higher price/lower output

Figure 17
Increased advertising: lower price/higher output

The usefulness of the theory of monopolistic competition

The theory of monopolistic competition was developed over 70 years ago in order to help explain a type of competition which lay somewhere between two extremes: perfect competition – where a large number of firms produce a **homogeneous good** or **service**, and monopoly – where a single enterprise controls the supply of a homogeneous good or service.

In these cases, the good or service was relatively easy to define. However in monopolistic competition, with its **heterogeneous** (differentiated) **good or service**, it is sometimes difficult to define the specific industry or competing group within which that certain good or service lies. For example, are toothpaste, dental floss, and toothpicks part of the same market or group? Similarly, should products such as coffee, tea, beer or wine be placed in the same group? Under perfect competition or monopoly these would be considered different homogeneous products. Therefore under monopolistic competition it is not clear where we draw the line between them.

Another difficulty is that differentiated products are not necessarily produced by *many different* companies, as is normally assumed in monopolistic competition. For example, in markets where there are strong brand preferences there may be a range of different types of products produced by a *few* firms. Companies such as Proctor and Gamble or Unilever operate in such diverse sectors as the food, household goods, health, beauty and cosmetics. They produce many types of differentiated goods and compete aggressively with one another e.g. Proctor and Gamble's washing powders Ariel Future and Daz Automatic competes with Unilever's Persil automatic and Persil New Generation. This means that the market for differentiated products and the significant emphasis on advertising, may be more oligopolistic in nature (i.e. competition amongst a few large firms – see Chapter 6) rather than monopolistic.

As we indicated previously, the monopolistic model of competition assumed there are many small / medium sized sellers of a product or service. As a result, a change in price by one seller has little effect on the price set by other sellers in the same market. However, if we take the example of small petrol stations, we could say that a change in price by one petrol garage may have little effect on most other petrol stations *across the country*, but would have a significant impact on petrol stations in its *immediate vicinity*. In other words, the market for petrol is segmented with petrol stations competing with their immediate neighbours in price or promotional effort. In this case, the most appropriate model may be that of oligopoly rather than monopolistic.

The fact that monopolistic competition is a 'hybrid' form of market structure lying somewhere between perfect competition and monopoly, has sometimes made it difficult to 'locate' the marketplace in practice. As a result, the models of monopoly or oligopoly are often used to describe how firms operate in practice.

The importance of the model of monopolistic competition is that it introduced the concept of a downward sloping demand curve resulting from the presence of differentiated products or services. It also showed that advertising and product differentiation can have costs i.e. each firm operated at less than the minimum point on the AC curve as seen in Figure 15(b).

This theory of 'excess capacity' which is found within the monopolistic model also stimulates us to think about the real world. For example, although the firm under monopolistic competition produces at a higher than minimum average cost (AC) because the sloping demand curve (differentiated product) cuts the average cost curve to the left of the minimum point of the AC curve, this may be acceptable because consumers are prepared to pay more for choice. Also, as we have seen above, there are examples where advertising has actually led to a decrease in the ultimate price of goods and services.

Despite these interesting aspects of monopolistic competition, it is often felt that the role which *strategy* plays in the real business world is most often seen in highly concentrated markets where a small number of powerful large firms compete with one another. In this situation, a company has to think about the potential reactions of its few rivals before it decides on any change in its price or other variables. It is to this interesting strategic marketplace of oligopoly that we now turn.

KEY WORDS

Product differentiation	Specialisation strategy
Excess capacity	Homogenous good or service
Concentration ratio	Heterogeneous good or service
Concentrated industries	Strategic marketplace

Further reading

Grant, S. and Vidler, C., Part 2 Unit 2 in *Economics in Context*, Heinemann Educational Publishers, 2000.

Griffiths, A. and Wall, S., Chapter 6 in *Intermediate Micro Economics*, 2nd edn, Longman, 2000.

Ison, S., Chapter 7 in *Economics*, 3rd edn, Financial Times/Prentice Hall, 2000.

Sloman, J., Chapter 7 in *Economics*, 4th edn, Prentice Hall Europe, 2000.

Useful websites

Advertising Association: www.adassoc.org.uk/
Design Council: www.design-council.org.uk/
Financial Times: www.ft.co.uk
The Guardian: www.guardian.co.uk/archive

Essay topics

1. (a) Explain the characteristics of a monopolistically competitive market. [10 marks]
   (b) Compare monopolistic competition and perfect competition. [10 marks]
2. 'Monopolistic competition benefits consumers.' Evaluate this statement. [20 marks]

Data response question

This task is based on a question set by OCR in November 1999. Read the piece below then study Table A and the two extracts. Answer the questions that follow using this material and the principles you have learnt from this chapter.

A proposed new out-of-town superstore

Lower Sandford is a market town situated in a rural part of southern England and is surrounded by several small villages. It has an old centre and narrow streets, and is characterised by a large number of independent retailers who cater for local residents and tourists. There are two small supermarkets situated in the town centre and these compete with other retailers who sell similar sorts of products.

This pattern of retailing may be set to change significantly with the proposal by a large supermarket chain to build a new superstore a mile from the town centre. The town council is currently considering whether to grant planning permission for this new superstore. The following information is being considered by the council in an effort to reach its decision.

A report from local retailers

This report, commissioned by a group of local retailers, concentrates on concerns about the possible impact upon their trade of the new superstore. It concludes:

- Any fall in trade will cause job losses.
- Sales of all products will be affected, depending on the prices charges by the superstore. For example, Table A shows the possible impact on demand for loaves of bread sold by local retailers, depending on the price charged by the superstore for its bread. The assumptions are:
  1. The current average price of a loaf of bread in the town is £1.00.
  2. Weekly sales currently average about 2500 loaves.
  3. Local retailers hold their price of £1.00 per loaf constant.

Table A The impact of the superstore on bread sales

Estimated weekly demand of loaves from **local retailers**	Price charged by **new superstore** per loaf
2000	£1.00
1600	£0.90
1200	£0.80
800	£0.70
400	£0.60

A report from the national supermarket chain applying for planning permission

This report stresses the various benefits that the new superstore will bring to the local area. In particular, the supermarket chain emphasises:

- The benefit of lower prices on a range of products due to the economics od scale available to a supermarket chain.
- The creation of approximately 200 new jobs at the superstore.
- The provision of a free bus to the superstore from certain pick-up points near the town centre.

1. (a) Explain what is meant by monopolistic competition. [3 marks]
    (b) Prior to the proposed opening of the superstore, to what extent can the retailing structure in Lower Sandford be described as an example of monopolistic competition? [5 marks]
2. (a) Define cross elasticity of demand. [2 marks]
    (b) Suppose the proposed superstore, once operating, were to change the price of its loaves from £1.00 to £0.80.
    (i) Using Table A, calculate the cross elasticity of demand for loaves of bread sold by local retailers with regard to the price of loaves sold by the proposed superstore if the superstore were to cut its price in this way. [2 marks]
        (ii) Explain what the figure you have calculated means t economist. [4 marks]
    (c) Using supply and demand analysis, explain *two* possible ways in which local retailers of loaves of bread might respond to the likely fall in their sales. [6 marks]

Chapter Six

Oligopoly

'In duels of strategy you must move the opponent's attitude. Attack where his spirit is lax, throw him into confusion, irritate and terrify him. Take advantage of the enemy's rhythm when he is unsettled and you can win.'
Musashi Miyamoto, seventeenth century Japanese samurai

Introduction

This chapter deals with an oligopolistic market structure in which a few firms dominate the industry. In such a market, firms recognize their **interdependence**, and are aware that their actions are likely to encourage counter-action by their rivals. Therefore, any theory of oligopoly has to take account of the fact that firms in such a market are rivals and interdependent. Oligopolistic markets are intermediate between that of perfect competition and monopoly.

This chapter has three aims. First it deals with the method of measuring the degree of oligopoly in a market – that is, the *concentration ratio*. Secondly, it outlines a number of models of oligopolistic behaviour, starting with the *non-collusive* models of the kinked demand curve and game theory, before dealing with the *collusive* models of price leadership. Finally, the chapter deals with non-price competition, which is a feature of oligopolistic markets.

Non-collusive oligopoly is a situation in which firms act independently of each other whilst still recognizing their interdependence. Collusive oligopoly involves agreement between firms, both formal (e.g. cartels) and informal (e.g. tacit agreements).

The concentration ratio

As you saw in Chapter 4, it is normally the case that monopoly power arises when there are relatively few firms in the industry. However, it is not simply a matter of how many firms there are in a particular market but the number of *major players* in that market.

For example, 80 per cent of a market may be concentrated in the hands of five major players, whereas another market may consist of more firms but 80 per cent of the market may be concentrated in the hands of just two firms (which is called a **duopoly**). The degree of concentration can be measured by what is known as a **concentration**

Table 10 Five-firm concentration ratios for certain industrial groups

Industrial group	Net output (%)	Employment (%)
Tobacco	99	98
Motor vehicles and their engines	84	80
Cement, lime and plaster	80	82
Ice-cream, cocoa, chocolate and sugar confectionery	73	61
Pharmaceutical products	51	32
Footwear	48	44
Brewing and malting	38	45
Printing and publishing	16	13

Source: Adapted from Griffiths and Wall, *Applied Economics*, 2001

ratio which shows the proportion of output or employment in a given industry accounted for by, say, the three, four or five largest firms. Table 10 illustrates five-firm concentration ratios for certain industries.

It is obvious that some industries are more dominated by large firms than are other industries. For example, the five largest firms in the tobacco industry account for 99 per cent of net output and 98 per cent of employment. In printing and publishing, however, the five largest firms account for only 16 and 13 per cent respectively for net output and employment.

Video game consoles

The video game market consists of two segments – the hardware sector producing consoles, and the software market, which comprises the games that are played on the consoles. There are many software companies, with something in the region of 60–70 in the UK alone. In 1999 the console market was composed of only three manufacturers – Sega, Nintendo and Sony. In 1999 their market shares were estimated to be 3, 27 and 70 per cent respectively. This is a clear example of an oligopolistic market with a three-firm concentratio ratio of 100 per cent.

The market is growing and you would expect this to attract new firms. However, the market possesses significant barriers to entry – not least the technological requirements, the existence of economies of scale and the high start-up costs.

Interdependence in oligopolistic markets

Oligopoly is a market structure in which there are only a few firms operating in a given sector or industry. The market share of each firm is sufficiently large that decisions taken by one firm will affect the decisions taken by the other firms in the market. The theory of oligopoly has to take into account how many firms operate in a marketplace where there is great rivalry and interdependence.

Oligopolistic conditions exist when one of the firms in the market anticipates the **reaction** of the other firms in the market and changes its behaviour according to how it thinks the other firms will react. In the perfectly competitive market structure outlined in Chapter 3, each firm was a *price-taker* so that no one firm had any effect on the other firms. In the *pure* monopoly situation outlined in Chapter 4 there is only one firm and therefore the monopolist acts as a *price-maker*.

The situation outlined above makes it difficult to develop an adequate theory of oligopolistic markets because the strategy which one firm takes will depend on how it feels its competitors will react. Nevertheless there are a number of theories which attempt to explain oligopolistic behaviour. Two such theories are the *kinked demand curve theory* and *game theory*. These can be used as an illustration of interdependence between firms in oligopolistic markets.

Kinked demand curve theory

The **kinked demand curve** can be used to explain how, in oligopolistic markets where a few firms dominate, prices tend to be stable for substantial periods; i.e. the price is often rigid (price rigidity). The model is illustrated in Figure 18.

It is assumed that the firm is producing output Q and charging a price of P. Given the fact that interdependence exists in oligopolistic markets, the firm naturally thinks that if it increases its price above P other firms in the market will *not* follow. The reason for this is the belief that the other firms will keep their price fixed in order to attract consumers away from the firm that has raised its prices. Thus an oligopolist perceives its demand curve as being relatively elastic in response to an *increase* in price. As a result the demand curve is represented by AB with a marginal revenue curve of AC.

On the other hand, if the firm lowers its price below P it assumes that other firms in the market will do likewise so as not to lose market share to that firm. Hence a 'price war' is started. In such a situation, the firm expects the demand curve to be relatively inelastic in response to a price decrease, with a demand curve represented by BD and a marginal revenue curve of EF.

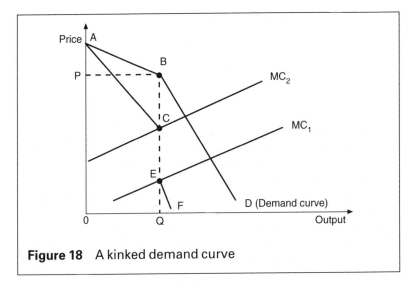

Figure 18 A kinked demand curve

Overall, therefore, the oligopolist believes it is facing a demand curve that is kinked, namely ABD in Figure 18. There is no incentive to increase or decrease price so that the price will thus be rigid at P.

From the above account, we can see that the oligopolist will face a marginal revenue curve represented by ACEF with a discontinuity between C and E. This discontinuity can also be seen as another reason for price rigidity because the oligopolist's marginal cost can increase from MC_1 to MC_2 without affecting either output or price.

Although the kinked demand curve theory is useful as a theory of oligopolistic behaviour, it is not without shortcomings. Price rigidity may not be the result of the kinked demand curve theory, but rather because it is often too expensive to continually change prices. The theory has been criticized for not being a theory at all. The reason for this is that it doesn't explain *how* price P is achieved – only why, once set, it is likely not to move from that position. Empirical evidence suggests that prices in oligopolistic markets are often no more rigid than in other market situations.

Game theory

As stated in the introduction, a major feature of oligopolistic markets is the interdependence between a few firms who are constantly trying to identify their rival's reactions to changes they make. Interdependence can be analysed by the use of **game theory**.

Figure 19 is a **pay-off matrix**. It shows two firms, X and Y, each having

		Firm Y's strategy			
		Advertising		Price-cutting	
Firm X's strategy	Advertising	8	8	16	0
	Price-cutting	0	16	12	12

Figure 19   Pay-off matrix in terms of profit (£m)

two strategies – advertising and price-cutting. The matrix is expressed in terms of profit, with the left side of each box referring to firm X's profit and the right side to firm Y's profit. Thus if firm X undertakes an advertising strategy and firm Y decides on a price-cutting strategy, then firm X receives £16 million profit and firm Y zero profit.

Given the pay-off matrix, the two firms can determine their **optimum strategy**, with each firm recognizing its dependence on the other. Thus, firm X will decide on advertising as its strategy since at best this could lead to a profit of £16 million (assuming firm Y chooses the price-cutting strategy) or at worst lead to a profit of £8 million (if Y chooses to advertise). If firm X had chosen a price cutting strategy, then the best it could have achieved is a profit of £12 million (if Y had also chosen a price-cutting strategy) and the worst would have been no profit at all (if Y had chosen to advertise). As such, firm X has a **dominant strategy**, which is to advertise, since X will adopt this strategy whatever strategy Y adopts, because its profit will be £8 million or £16 million as opposed to zero or £12 million.

If we next consider firm Y, the same outcome will be achieved since Y will adopt advertising as its dominant strategy. The reason for this is that if Y were to choose advertising as its strategy, it would either obtain profit of £8 million (if X were also to advertise) or £16 million (if X were to price-cut). Alternatively, if firm Y were to price-cut, it would either obtain zero profit (if X were to advertise) or £12 million (if X were to price-cut). Thus firm Y, faced with either £8 million or £16 million if it advertises or zero or £12 million if it price-cuts, it will choose the advertising strategy. With this being the case there is an equilibrium with both firms advertising and each earning profit of £8 million (the top left-hand box in the matrix).

Figure 19 clearly illustrates that each firm could have obtained more profit (£12 million) by both adopting a price-cutting strategy (the bottom right-hand box in the matrix). However, this would not be achieved independently since one or other of the two firms could find themselves with zero profit. It would be achieved only if the two firms *colluded*. **Collusion** is the area we now turn to.

Collusive oligopoly

The kinked demand curve theory and game theory are both non-collusive models of oligopoly. This means that each firm has decided on its own strategy without colluding with the other firms in the market. However, game theory does reveal that the two firms could have achieved higher profits (namely £12 million each) if they had worked together, that is colluded. Given the benefits derived from such collusive behaviour, the government seeks to control the creation of excessive profits through *competition policy*. That is covered in Chapter 9.

Collusion can take a number of forms. **Formal collusion** is where firms may seek to organize themselves into a *cartel,* using some form of centralized body in order to coordinate the setting of price and output in order to maximize the profits of the members of the cartel.

Cartels are illegal in the UK, so if collusion does take place it is more likely to be **tacit collusion**. This is where firms cooperate, but not in a formal manner. The most common form of tacit collusion is **price leadership**, in which one firm in the oligopolistic market sets the price and the others follow. Price leadership can take a number of forms.

Dominant-firm price leadership

In this situation a dominant firm is often the price leader in an oligopolistic market. This firm may control a major share of the industry output and may be seen by the other firms as the price-setter. As such, the dominant firm will set the price and the other firms in the market will follow, in order to avoid a price war.

In explaining this model of price leadership we assume that the oligopolistic market consists of one **dominant firm** that wishes to maximize profits, and many other smaller firms who are price-takers.

In Figure 20 the *total* market demand is shown, as is the supply curve for *all the small firms in the industry*. From the market demand curve it is possible to derive the demand curve for the dominant firm. At a price of P_1 the small firms would be able to supply the whole market, so there would be no demand for the dominant firm's product. However, if the price were P_2 then the small firms would not supply anything and so the dominant firm would have the market to itself.

It is possible to construct the demand curve for the dominant firm, which is P_1D_L in Figure 21. The dominant firm's demand curve is the difference between the market demand curve and what the smaller firms are willing to supply at each and every price. Given the dominant firm's demand curve, its marginal revenue curve can be seen as MR_L. Since it was stated that the dominant firm is a profit-maximizer, then with a marginal cost curve of MC_L it will produce

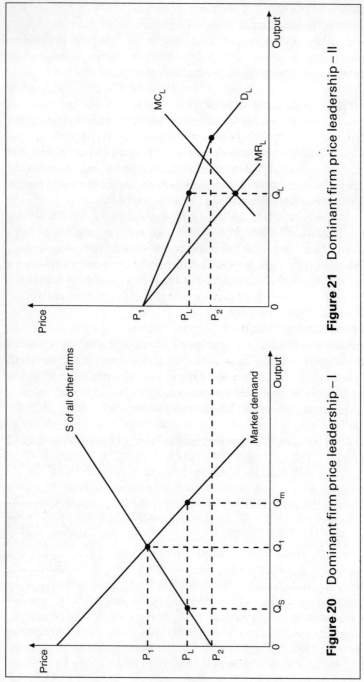

Figure 21 Dominant firm price leadership – II

Figure 20 Dominant firm price leadership – I

Q_L (where $MC_L = MR_L$) and charge a price of P_L. This price having been set by the dominant firm, all other firms in the oligopolistic market will follow and supply the amount Q_S. The overall quantity demanded (Q_m) at a price of P_L is $Q_L + Q_S$. It is the amount demanded from the dominant firm and the small firms respectively.

Barometric-firm price leadership

In this situation the price leader is not the dominant firm in the market. The price leader may in fact be a small firm but one that has a close knowledge of the market. Such a firm is known as a **barometric firm** since it is particularly sensitive to market movements and may, therefore, instigate a price change, which the other firms in the oligopolistic market often follow.

Low-cost price leadership

A **low-cost firm** may establish itself as the price leader in the market. Other firms in the market whose costs are higher choose to follow the price leadership of the low-cost firm for fear of encouraging a price war which could ultimately lead to them being forced out of the market.

Non-price competition

It is important to note that competition by means other than price occurs in oligopolistic markets because of the *potential* for price wars. **Non-price competition** may take a number of forms, such as promotional offers. Advertising can also be used in order to create a brand image. Table 11 shows the amount spent by UK advertisers in 2000.

Table 11 The top ten UK advertisers in terms of spending in 2000

Rank	Organization	Advertising Spend 2000 (£)
1	Proctor & Gamble	122,617,597
2	BT	107,809,663
3	COI Communications	102,747,590
4	Renault	70,638,391
5	L'Oreal	59,738,197
6	Vauxhall Motors	57,071,973
7	Ford Motor Co.	55,852,708
8	Van den Bergh	51,707,336
9	British Sky Broadcasting	47,977,727
10	Vodafone	47,781,696

Source: Adapted from *Marketing*, 15 March 2001

Free flight promotion

Hoover launched a free flight promotion in 1992 as a means of stimulating demand and gaining market share at the expense of its competitors' products. Customers who spent a minimum of £100 on the purchase of one of its products qualified for two free return flights to one of six European destinations. This was subsequently extended to include US destinations ...

The aim of any promotion is to expand the sale of the product, thus increasing revenue and to strengthen brand loyalty by means of non-price competition. The Hoover promotion was successful in terms of the level of demand it generated, but it created a number of difficulties.

First, additional labour had to be employed and the factory had to be placed on 7-day working in order to meet the increased demand for appliances. Second, it soon became apparent that consumers where buying the product for the free flight offer rather than for the product itself. This is evident by advertisements, which began to appear in the second-hand section of local newspapers and Exchange and Mart for Hoover appliances, mainly vacuum cleaners, which had been bought but never used. This was hardly a policy aimed at improving brand loyalty. Third, the offer exceeded all expectations and thus proved to be a costly promotion.

With all promotions it is forecast that a good percentage of those buying the product will not actually take up the promotional offer for which they are eligible. For travel-related promotions it is estimated that the level of take-up is 10 per cent or below. In terms of the Hoover promotion a higher than expected number of consumers took up the offer ...

With hindsight, Hoover could have possibly made the offer more restrictive. For example, they could have set the point of eligibility at £200 rather than £100, or offered only one free ticket rather than two. In many promotions the customer has to apply for the offer of a free gift and this often involves them in having to make additional purchases such as hotel accommodation or restaurant meals. This would have proved to be an additional cost to the consumer and could ultimately have acted as a deterrent to taking advantage of the free flight offer.

In recent years it is certainly the case that non-price competition in the form of promotional activity incorporating offers such as the use of free air miles, air tickets or holidays have become more popular. However, any promotional activity includes an element of risk for the company ...

Source: Adapted from the *British Economy Survey*, vol. 24, autumn 1994

The table reveals heavy advertising by organizations that produce a range of brands. For example, Proctor & Gamble produce the detergents Ariel, Bold and Daz as well as Pampers Nappies and Always, whereas Van den Bergh produce PG Tips and Flora margarine.

Promotional offers can take a number of forms, such as 'buy two, get one free', 25 per cent extra free or free gifts. One such free gift offer is outlined in the box 'Free flight promotion'. This also highlights the dangers of such a promotion.

KEY WORDS

Interdependence	Collusion
Duopoly	Formal collusion
Concentration ratio	Tacit collusion
Reaction	Price leadership
Kinked demand curve	Dominant firm
Game theory	Barometric firm
Pay-off matrix	Low-cost firm
Optimum strategy	Non-price competition
Dominant strategy	

Further reading

Grant, S., Chapter 43 in *Stanlake's Introductory Economics*, 7th edn, Longman, 2000.

Griffiths, A. and Wall, S., Chapters 8 and 9 in *Intermediate Microeconomics*, 2nd edn, Financial Times/Prentice Hall, 2000.

Griffiths, A. and Wall, S. (eds), Chapter 6 in *Applied Economics*, 9th edn, Financial Times/Prentice Hall, 2001.

Ison, S., Chapter 7 in *Economics*, 3rd edn, Financial Times/Prentice Hall, 2000.

Essay topics

1. (a) Using examples to illustrate your answer, explain the main features of oligopolistic markets. [12 marks]
   (b) Discuss the considerations a firm operating in an oligopolistic market is likely to take into account when deciding how much to spend on advertising. [13 marks]
   [AEB, January 1998]

2. (a) Explain why a firm's marginal cost of production is likely to be different in the short run and in the long run. [12 marks]
(b) Discuss the significance of production costs to a firm in an oligopolistic industry when fixing the price it charges for its product. [13 marks]
[AEB, June 1997]

Data response question

This task is based on a question set by AQA in 2000. Read the piece below, which is adapted from *First Report on Vehicle Pricing of the House of Commons Select Committee on Trade and Industry*, as well as Table A. Then answer the questions that follow.

The UK Car Market

There are around 40 vehicle manufacturers and importers operating in the UK. Around two million new cars are sold per year, mainly through a network of around 7000 authorized dealers. Car manufacturers enter into 'selective and exclusive' distribution agreements with their dealers. These allow the manufacturers to set standards which dealers must meet in return for an exclusive territory within which to operate.

In February 1998, the European Commission (EC) reported that the UK was the most expensive market for 61 of the 72 best-selling models in the European Union. The current price differentials between the UK and other EU countries are far beyond those regarded by the EC as acceptable. We believe that price discrimination might be responsible for some of these differences.

Price discrimination is possible because 'parallel importing', which occurs when consumers buy cars from dealers in other EU countries rather than from a manufacturer's authorized UK dealer, is more difficult in the UK than in most other EU countries. This is partly because of the difficulties consumers face in importing cars owing to the right-hand drive specification. UK consumers are also discouraged from buying their cars from other EU countries by the obvious practical inconvenience, primarily distance as they cannot drive over a border to take advantage of lower prices as some other European consumers can. Also, a recent ruling of the European Court of Justice limits 'grey imports' into the UK. 'Grey imports' include cars which are brought into the country through channels not approved by the manufacturers.

UK car buyers who wish to 'parallel import' may find that a request for a right-hand drive car from a continental dealer causes delay and difficulties. In February 1998, the EC stated that it was 'receiving continual complaints from British consumers who wished to purchase right-hand drive vehicles in the cheaper markets'. It went on to remind manufacturers that they must supply right-hand drive cars to any EU dealer wishing to sell them. Recently, VW was fined £67 million in January 1998 by the European Commission for forcing its authorized dealers in Italy to refuse to sell cars to foreign buyers. Circumstantial evidence at least would indicate that this is not a practice peculiar to VW.

The car manufacturers deny that price discrimination occurs and argue that other factors are responsible for price differences. These factors include exchange rates, tax rates, delivery costs, and the fact that a car sold in the UK is different from a car sold on the continent.

The UK is unusual in two further respects. Firstly, the company car of fleet car market represents over 70 per cent of new car sales. Manufacturers charge much higher prices and make much larger profits on cars sold to private motorists than they do on fleet cars sold to companies. Secondly, the UK has the biggest used car market in Europe, in part because of the size of the UK fleet sector. Lower list prices for new cars in the UK would have an adverse effect on the used car market. Manufacturers are keen to keep high prices for new cars to protect second-hand values since high second-hand values improve the attraction of the car for consumers. Part of the new-car pricing policy involves 'protecting' second-hand car prices.

Table A UK new car registrations in 1997

Manufacturer	Share (%)	Manufacturer	Share (%)
Ford group (Ford, Jaguar)	18.7	Renault	7.3
General Motors (Vauxhall, Opel, Saab)	14.3	Nissan	4.4
BMW group (BMW, Rover)	12.9	Fiat group (Fiat, Alfa Romeo)	4.3
Peugeot group (Peugeot, Citroen)	11.4	Toyota	3.3
Volkswagen group (VW, Audi, Seat, Skoda)	8.7	Others	14.7

1. (a) Making use of the article and Table A, describe the market structure of the car industry in the UK. [4 marks]

   (b) From the article, identify *two* entry barriers, and explain briefly how they affect the structure and competitiveness of the UK car market. [6 marks]

2. (a) Explain how price discrimination might be responsible for some of the differences in car prices between the UK and other EU countries. [10 marks]

   (b) Discuss whether price discrimination provides an adequate explanation of the different prices charged in the UK car market compared with other EU countries. [30 marks]

Chapter Seven

Contestable markets

'Nevertheless, I must resist the temptation to describe the analysis I will report here as anything like a revolution; perhaps terms such as "rebellion" and "uprising" are the more apt.'
William J Baumol

What is a contestable market?

'Contestable markets' is a recent theory of market structure which is based on the likely effect which potential new entrants could have on the price and output decisions of firms already in the market (**incumbent firms**).

A *contestable market* is a market structure in which entry into an industry is free and exit is costless. Even the *threat* of new firm entry causes incumbent firms to act as though such potential entry actually exists. Instead of regarding competitive behaviour as existing only in a perfectly or monopolistically competitive market, it could exist in markets which are contestable.

The notion of contestability was developed by the American economist William Baumol. He considered the case of an unregulated airline route. Even if an airline operator were the only one on a particular route it would not be able to charge excessive fares. If it did, new operators would enter the market. There would be no irrecoverable costs, because new operations can lease their aircraft. Even if they were purchased, they could still be sold if the operator decided to leave the market.

Like perfect competition, and to a certain extent monopoly, contestable markets are not so much a description of the real world but rather a benchmark against which other theories of market behaviour can be assessed.

Free entry and exit from the market

Free entry to a market means that potential entrants are not at a disadvantage as compared with incumbent firms in terms of:

- having to suffer higher costs

- having consumers prefer the products of other firms

- lacking access to equivalent production technology.

For example, if potential entrants into an industry are not able to gain access to the same type of technology as that used by the incumbent firms, that will prevent such new entrants from competing on the same terms with respect to costs or quality. This inability to access the same type of technology would restrict the threat of potential entrants, and would permit incumbents to earn supernormal profits in the long run.

Similarly, extensive branding by incumbent firms could also decrease the threat of new entrants and thus permit the incumbents to earn supernormal profits.

However, the absence of entry barriers means that it is easier for new firms to enter the market. The existence of this threat is assumed to reduce any tendency of incumbent firms to increase their prices significantly above their average costs, thus earning supernormal profit. Generally speaking, the fewer the barriers to entry into a market, the more contestable that market is.

Costless exit means that firms can leave the industry without a financial penalty. This means they have no **sunk costs**, since the capital they invested when they entered the industry can be resold without loss.

The concept of sunk costs is an important aspect of the theory of contestable markets. If exit were not costless then it would act effectively as a cost of entry. All this means that potential entrants are not put off from entering a market by the possibility that existing firms engage in price cuts, because new entrants can always leave the industry without financial penalty.

As a result, contestable markets experience **hit and run entry**. The attraction of supernormal profits leads new firms to enter a market, obtain a share of the profits, and then leave the industry when profits have been taken. It is also the case that the threat of potential entry encourages existing firms to be efficient (e.g. to minimize their costs of production in order to deter entry of other firms).

Sunk costs

Sunk costs are the cost of acquiring an asset, such as a piece of machinery, which cannot be recouped by selling the machinery or using it in another market if the firm exits the industry. If sunk costs *do* exist they increase the cost of leaving the industry and make the incumbent firms more determined to avoid being forced out of the industry. In other words, the existence of sunk costs makes incumbent firms more aggressive towards new entrants, leading them to adopt a number of strategies that act as a barrier to entry to new firms.

Perfectly contestable markets

If there is a complete absence of barriers to entry into a market, and if exit from that market is costless, then the market is said to be **perfectly contestable**. These conditions will ensure that incumbents are not able to earn supernormal profits in the long run.

Thus the price charged in the market will equate to long-run average cost. If a price is charged above long-run average cost, a new firm will be attracted into the market which will undercut the price charged by incumbents. Since the new entrant can leave the market at zero cost, such 'hit and run' tactics mean that they can earn supernormal profits in the period before the incumbents react and lower their own prices.

A contestable market would appear to be similar to a *perfectly competitive market*, and it is true that perfectly competitive markets are also perfectly contestable. The reverse is not true, however, since a contestable market could be one in which only a few firms exist. In a contestable market the size and number of firms will be determined by the market. In perfectly contestable markets, therefore, there are no barriers to entry. As a result, firms:

- are cost efficient

- earn only normal profits in the long run

- cannot cross-subsidize between products

- cannot set prices below costs in order to deter new entrants

- are constrained to keep their prices at levels that (taking account of costs) earn only normal profits.

Less restrictive assumptions

Interest in the contestable market model stems from the fact that it has less restrictive assumptions than the perfectly competitive model, which is often seen as the ideal market structure.

The assumptions for perfect competition, contestability and monopoly are given in Table 12. It reveals that the assumptions made about contestable markets are less restrictive than made about the other two, not least in terms of the size and number of firms and product homogeneity. Even monopolistic or oligopolistic markets could, in principle, experience a high degree of contestability, so long as entry is free and exit is costless.

It is more realistic to imagine an industry approaching perfect contestability than perfect competition, especially given the assumption about price-takers. In contestable markets there is no

Table 12 Assumptions of perfect competition, contestable markets and monopoly

Assumptions	Perfect competition	Perfectly contestable	Pure monopoly
Objective of the firm	Profit maximization	Profit maximization	Profit maximization
Barriers to entry and exit	None	None	High
Number of firms	Many	Doesn't matter	One
Price-takers	Yes	Not required	No
Size of firms	Small	Doesn't matter	Large
Product homogeneity	Yes	Not necessarily	Yes
Profits in the long run	Normal	Normal	Supernormal

requirement for a large number of small, price-taking firms operating in the industry as in perfect competition. What is central in terms of contestable market theory is the freedom of firms to enter or exit the industry without incurring any costs.

As stated above, the essence of contestable markets is that there exists the potential for hit and run entry – that is, firms can freely enter an industry, reap the profits that are available, then leave the industry without incurring any costs when the opportunity for profits disappear.

The notion of contestable markets has been seen to be applicable to certain parts of the service sector, particularly if capital equipment is rented. As such, it has been seen to have relevance to the transport sector and in particular the road haulage industry, the airline industry

New-age electronics

Once, to be a big consumer-electronics firm meant building and operating huge factories in low-cost parts of the world. Now this work is increasingly outsourced to contract manufacturers, such as Flextronics and Solectron (which recently bought two factories from Sony). These companies will work for anyone, allowing even the smallest start-up to manufacture devices on the same production line as, say, Panasonic. New-age consumer-electronics firms, such as Palm and Handspring, do not have a single factory between them, despite shipping tens of millions of devices. The rise of the contract manufacturer has lowered the barrier to entry into the business dramatically.

Extract from *The Economist*, 8 March 2001

and local bus provision. In fact, deregulation of the local bus market was actually based on the assumption that the market was contestable.

In these markets, capital can be easily rented for a short period and exit poses few costs.

Problems with contestability

Although it has been stated that airline operators could be considered to undertake their business in a contestable market, commentators such as Griffiths and Wall cast doubt on this view.

The policy implications would suggest the removal of entry barriers and the lowering of exit costs in all market structures as a way of increasing the level of contestability.

Contestability and barriers to entry in the airline industry

- Sunk costs are more prevalent in the airline industry than once recognized. For example, it is recognized that advertising costs need to be high in order to persuade travellers to switch to new airlines. As such, it would take an airline company both time and money to determine whether a new service is likely to be profitable.
- Even though the sunk costs within the airline industry are smaller than in other industries, there are other barriers to entry. For example, airport landing slots are limited by both time and physical space, such that large incumbent airlines often possess most of the slots. In addition, *frequent flyer* initiatives by incumbents (whereby those who extensively use the airline are rewarded with free flights) ensure customer loyalty which new entrants could not exploit.
- *Hit and run* potential within contestable markets is difficult if existing firms can quickly lower their prices to compete with newcomers.
- The assumption that the *threat* of competition is sufficient to control market behaviour can be questioned. It would be fair to say that it is *actual* rather than potential entry, which influence behaviour.
- The observed outbreaks of price wars among airline operators would suggest that it is *actual* competition, rather than potential competition, that keeps profits at a reasonable level.

Source: Adapted from Griffiths and Wall (2000)

Conclusion

It is difficult to give any real-world examples of contestable markets because in many industries there are often sunk costs which are not recoverable when firms exit the industry. The theory does, however, indicate that the structure of a market and how firms behave within that market cannot be determined just by counting the number of firms in the industry.

KEY WORDS

Incumbent firms	Sunk cost
Free entry	Hit and run entry
Costless exit	Perfectly contestable

Further reading

Anderton, A., Unit 58 in *Economics*, 3rd edn, Causeway Press, 2000.

Griffiths, A. and Wall, S., Chapter 6 in *Intermediate Economics*, 2nd edn, Financial Times/Prentice Hall, 2000.

Ison, S., Chapter 7 in *Economics*, 3rd edn, Financial Times/Prentice Hall, 2000.

Sloman, J., Chapter 6 in *Economics*, 4th edn, Financial Times/Prentice Hall, 2000.

Essay topics

1. (a) Explain briefly the meaning of the terms 'barriers to entry' and 'barriers to exit'. [30 marks]

   (b) How might barriers to entry be expected to affect the way in which markets operate in the real world? Illustrate your answer with relevant examples. [70 marks]

   [Edexcel, June 1996]

2. (a) Explain what is meant by a contestable market. [10 marks]

   (b) Discuss the extent to which the market for training shoes is contestable. [15 marks]

Data response question

This task is based on a question set by Edexcel in 2000. Study Tables A and B below and then, using your knowledge of economics, answer the questions that follow.

Table A National newspaper circulation in the UK

Title of newspaper	Owned by	Daily circulation		
		1992	*1993*	*1994*
The Sun	News Corporation	3,588,077	3,513,591	4,007,520
Daily Mirror	Headington Investment	2,868,263	2,676,015	2,484,436
Daily Mail	Daily Mail	1,688,808	1,769,253	1,784,030
Daily Express	United Newspapers	1,537,726	1,490,323	1,369,266
Daily Telegraph	Ravelston Corporation	1,043,703	1,024,340	1,007,944
Daily Star	United Newspapers	808,486	773,908	746,412
Today	News Corporation	495,405	533,332	579,110
The Guardian	Guardian Newspapers	418,026	416,207	400,399
The Times	News Corporation	390,323	368,219	471,847
The Independent	Newspaper Publishing	376,532	348,692	284,440
Financial Times	Pearson	291,915	290,139	296,984
Totals		13,507,264	13,204,019	13,433,188

Table B Prices of the following were reduced in early 1993

Newspaper	Old price	New price
The Sun	25 pence	20 pence
The Times	45 pence	20 pence
Daily Telegraph	48 pence	30 pence

1. With reference to Table A, comment on the view that News Corporation was a monopoly in the market for national newspapers in 1994 [5 marks]
2. Discuss *two* reasons why some newspaper companies publish more than one newspaper title. [6 marks]
3. Some of the other newspaper publishers considered that the price reductions announced by News Corporation for *The Sun* and *The Times* were an example of predatory pricing.
   (a) Analyse the meaning of the term 'predatory pricing'. [5 marks]
   (b) Examine *three* reasons which might explain why News Corporation embarked on such a pricing policy. [9 marks]
4. To what extent might newspaper publishing be regarded as a contestable market? [9 marks]
5. In the UK, newspaper publishers are prevented from controlling domestic independent television companies. Why might newspaper publishers seek to expand into other media? [6 marks]

Chapter Eight

Pricing and the market

'Everything is worth what its purchaser will pay for it.'
Publilius Synus, Roman writer, first century BC

General factors determining price

Basically, price is the amount of money charged for goods or services. In other words it is the value, in money terms, which a consumer exchanges for the benefits or satisfaction of using the good or service.

In the marketing context, price is said to be one of the constituents of the **marketing mix** which also includes quality, design, advertising, marketing and distribution.

There are many factors which have a bearing on how entrepreneurs finally decide on their pricing strategy. They may be classified into two broad categories – internal and external.

Internal factors

One of the most basic internal factors determining the price charged for a good or service is the actual *objectives* the firm is pursuing. The objectives might be one of the following.

- *Maximize current profits.* In this case, firms often set a higher price for a product because consumers are willing to pay that price – that is, the demand is relatively inelastic. The firm can then distribute profits to the shareholders to keep them satisfied.

- *Maximize market share.* In this situation, a firm often sets price as low as possible in the belief that a larger share of the market will enable it to lower unit costs via economies of scale, thus maximizing long-run profits.

- *Product quality leadership.* Here the company may charge a higher price than normal in an attempt to convince customers that the higher price is worth the extra because of the product's superior quality or reliability.

A second internal factor affecting price determination is the *marketing mix strategy*. For example, if a company manager decides to base the sales of the product on non-price factors such as design and promotion, then these will strongly affect the pricing decision.

A third internal factor which affects the pricing decision is costs of production. Costs often set the floor for prices and many companies compete in the market by trying to be *low-cost producers*. In industries where costs can fall rapidly with output (i.e. where both economies of scale and learning curve effects are strong), then prices may be pushed down substantially.

Finally, one should not forget that prices are also affected by factors which are dependent on the internal organization of a firm. Some prices may be determined by a firm's head office while other companies may decide on locally determined prices. For example, the US company Gillette decides on the *average* price level for a given product in comparison with competing brands. At the same time, the managers of its worldwide subsidiaries are responsible for setting the *exact* price for that product – one that is suitable to their own specific geographical market.

External factors

Some external factors affect how prices are determined. For example, the pricing of goods and services depends on the nature of the market.

- *Monopolistic markets.* These markets contain many sellers of differentiated products, so the pricing decision will depend on how one firm tries to distinguish its own products from similar ones produced by other firms, through advertising and brand strategies.

- *Oligopolistic markets.* In these markets, where only a few sellers operate, the determination of prices is much more closely linked to competitors' strategies. For example, if one firm increases price and other firms do not follow, then that firm will lose customers rapidly.

- *Monopoly market.* When one firm dominates a market, then it might be tempted to take advantage of this power by pushing prices higher, or by charging a different price in different markets for the same product (price discrimination). For example, a few years ago, the French water company Evian sold its 8oz bottle of mineral water for around 50p while the same water put into its moisturising spray would be priced at £2.50. Sometimes a group of firms may operate a complex monopoly and charge different prices in different markets, as in the case of the European car market (see page 50).

Another factor related to this aspect is the influence of competitors on a company's pricing strategy. Most firms who operate in a competitive environment, whether under monopoly or oligopoly conditions, decide on their prices after conducting research on the prices and strategies of their close competitors.

Finally, one should not forget that more general economic factors may also help to determine prices. For example, firms have to limit their price increases if the economy is sluggish or when interest rates are high, since both these situations affect the desire and ability of consumers to buy goods and services.

The main practical approaches to product pricing
Three general methods are used by managers to set prices:

- *cost-based pricing* – where price determination tends to have a strong internal orientation and is largely based on the firm's cost structure.

- *competitor-orientated pricing* – where the major influence on prices is the strategy of competitors.

- *marketing-oriented pricing* – where the focus is on linking prices to the value or satisfaction that customers place on the product or service.

Cost-based pricing
There are many forms of cost-based pricing (or **cost-plus pricing**), but the typical ones involve two processes.

First, the firm estimates the *cost per unit* of the product, taking into consideration both fixed costs (overheads) and variable costs (direct costs) per unit. Because cost levels vary with output, the firm has to calculate costs based on some assumed level of output. For example firms often base costs on the assumption that it will be operating at about 75 per cent of its output capacity.

Second, the firm then adds a *mark-up* to the estimated average cost. This mark-up is meant to cover any of the firm's costs not previously accounted for in the original calculations, plus a profit. The mark-up can be expressed as:

$$\text{Mark-up (\%)} = 100 \times (\text{price} - \text{cost})/\text{cost}.$$

This can be rearranged to give:

$$\text{Price} = \text{cost} \times (100 + \text{mark-up})/100.$$

For example, if an economics book costs £10 to produce and the publisher requires a mark-up of 80 per cent, then the price charged will be:

$$£10 \times (100+80)/100 = £18.$$

In the above example all the costs have been included, so it is a **full-cost pricing** technique. Sometimes, the price is based only on the variable or direct costs, with a mark-up being added to these unit costs – that is **direct-cost pricing**. For example, when seats on an aircraft are empty then it might be better to sell those seats at a level which just covers the costs of fuel and labour rather then leaving them empty, since the aircraft has to travel to its destination in any case.

Some firms tend to use the **target-return pricing** method, whereby the mark-up is determined partly by the rate of return the company wishes to earn on the capital it has invested. In this case the relationship is:

$$P = L + R + K + F/Q + \pi A/Q$$

where

  P = the price per unit
  L = the unit labour cost
  R = the unit material cost
  K = the unit marketing cost
  F = total fixed costs
  Q = the number of units the firm plans to produce
  A = the total gross operating assets
  π = the desired profit rate on those assets.

For many years, General Motors of the US – which invests billions of dollars in capital equipment (operating assets) in order to produce cars – had the objective of earning a target rate of return (π) of 15 per cent on its invested capital. The mark-up per unit would be set at a level sufficient to cover the required return on assets – i.e. to cover $\pi A/Q$.

Problems with mark-up procedures

- They lead to an increase in price as sales fall, because costs are based on estimated output. For example, as sales fall, estimated output will also fall and unit costs will therefore rise – forcing prices (which are based on those costs) to rise. This may not be the best strategic pricing policy in some circumstances because it might be best to let prices *fall* in order to maintain market share.

- Secondly, the full-cost method does not really take into consideration the consumers' willingness to pay (i.e. the elasticity of demand), nor the way in which competitors' prices are moving.

- Direct-cost pricing is often criticized because it does not take into consideration the consumers' willingness to pay when business is buoyant, nor can it be used in the long run when fixed costs must also be covered if the firm is to survive.

Advantages of mark-up pricing

Despite the above criticisms, mark-up pricing based on costs is popular. There are various reasons for this:

- Sellers are more certain about costs than they are about demand, so they do not have to make frequent adjustments as demand changes.

- When most firms in an industry use this pricing system then price competition is minimized.

- Companies often feel that cost-based pricing is fairer to both buyers and sellers since sellers get a fair and steady return on their sales over time without taking advantage of buyers during periods when demand is high.

The fact that cost-based pricing is still popular has been confirmed by UK research. According to this, firms were approximately four times more likely to raise their price as a result of increases in costs as opposed to increases in demand, and to reduce their price as a result of decreases in costs rather than decrease in demand. Thus, cost-based pricing is widespread.

Competitor-based pricing

With competitor-based pricing, prices are determined mainly by the firm's assessment of its competitors' strategies. Some firms may set a price level which is designed either to prevent another firm entering the industry, or to drive a rival out of the industry once it has entered. These are limit pricing and predatory pricing respectively

Limit pricing

In the case of **limit pricing**, firms already in the industry (incumbent firms) set their price at the highest level possible without inducing new entry into the industry. In other words, the limit price is the price that is not quite high enough to induce the entry of new firms since they will not earn a profit. By preventing entry, the incumbent firm hopes to avoid sharing the market with new firms, thus ensuring for itself a long-term profit maximization position.

In some cases, limit pricing is also used by large companies to prevent the expansion of smaller companies who are *already* in an industry. Given these points, there are two general entry situations.

Deterring the entry of a high-cost firm

In this case, a new firm entering the industry has higher costs than the existing firms. This may be because of the smaller scale of production and the additional expense of advertising which the potential entrant has to incur in order to offset the consumer loyalty which the existing

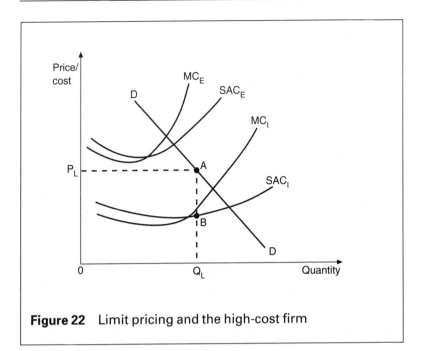

Figure 22 Limit pricing and the high-cost firm

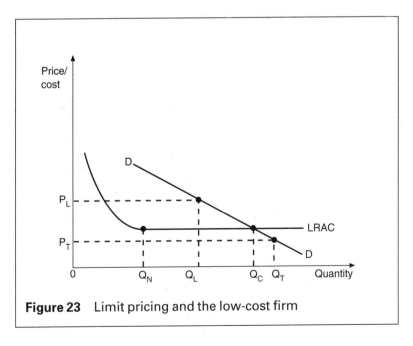

Figure 23 Limit pricing and the low-cost firm

companies have built up over time. The existing firms will then set a price which is less than the expected minimum cost per unit of the potential entrant firm.

In Figure 22 the entrant's short-run average cost curve (SAC_E) is seen to be above that of the incumbent firm (SAC_I). The incumbent firm will set a maximum price of P_L and reap a supernormal profit equal to AB per unit of sales at output Q_L. The entrant's curve SAC_E is above price P_L and it would thus trade at a loss if it entered the market.

Deterring the entry of a low-cost firm

In this case, the potential entrant has access to the same technology and factor markets as the existing firms so that the existing firms and the new entrants have the same costs. The existing firms choose a price such that if a new firm enters the market, the extra quantity it supplies will push the market price below the level of costs for all firms. The prospect of losses thus prevents new firms from entering the industry.

In Figure 23 both firms have an identical long-run average cost curve (LRAC), so the only barrier to entry for a new firm is the economies of scale barrier. In other words, a new firm will need to produce a minimum quantity of Q_N to enter the industry.

Knowing this, the incumbent produces quantity Q_L at the limit price P_L. This quantity is slightly larger than the difference between Q_C and Q_N, so that if the new entrant contemplates entry the total output would rise to Q_T (equal to $Q_N + Q_L$). That is, above the competitive output Q_C where LRAC cuts the market demand curve DD. This means that the price will fall to P_T which is below costs. In this way, by choosing to produce Q_L at a limit price of P_L, the incumbent firm seems to have managed to keep out new entrants.

Operating a limit-pricing strategy may be difficult because of a number of factors. Established firms may not have accurate information about the cost conditions of the potential entrants even in stable periods. As a result, they may find it difficult to discover the actual limit price and may have to proceed by trial and error. If there are a few firms already in the industry, then they may have to agree on sharing the market in such a way as to keep the price at the entry level. This may be difficult to do in practice. Rapidly changing demand and cost conditions in the industry will make it more difficult for established firms to calculate the limit price. New firms may have developed new products or processes which affect their costs and hence their ability to enter the industry.

The complexity of the limit-pricing system was seen during discussions in 2000 surrounding the merger between Alcan and Alusuisse, the Canadian and Swiss aluminium companies.

The two companies dominate the production of semi-rigid aluminium containers used by companies such as Mars and Nestlé for packaging their foods. The merger would affect smaller companies such as Teich, Pluspack and Alupack who also produce containers.

The European Commission's report on the merger noted that if companies such as Mars gave the smaller companies more orders then they would have had to invest in new equipment. However, this carried the risk that Alcan/Alusuisse would apply a limit-pricing strategy – i.e. charging prices which would be below what the smaller companies could afford given their commitment to high costs of new equipment.

Source: European Commission, Case No. Comp/M.1663

Predatory pricing

Predatory pricing is where an established firm reduces its price to below its rivals' costs of production (or in some instances below its own costs of production) over a certain period, in order to eliminate competition, or to strengthen its position in the market.

Predatory pricing is said to happen when a firm charges a price below short-run marginal costs of production, thus placing its rivals in financial difficulties. Since, in practice, it is sometimes difficult to measure marginal costs (MC), then predatory pricing is defined as a price which is below short-run average variable costs (AVC) – i.e. below direct costs.

This pricing strategy can also be used by a dominant firm as a means of disciplining rival firms who have increased their prices too much. This can be made even more effective if the dominant firm builds for itself a reputation for responding aggressively to new rivals.

In 2001, a clear case of predatory pricing was found to have been carried out in the UK by Napp Pharmaceuticals. It had sold its slow-release brand of morphine tablets called MST to hospitals at a 90 per cent discount off the official NHS list prices (see also page 50–1).

The Office of Fair Trading decided that the company had sold its 10mg, 30mg, 60mg and 100mg tablets at below direct costs in order to eliminate its three rival firms BIL, Link and Sanofi–Winthrop, from the market.

Source: Office of Fair Trading: Competition Act 1998 No. CA98/2D/2001

OFFICE OF FAIR TRADING

Newspaper pricing: News International gives assurances

21 May 1999 ... The agreement concludes an in-depth investigation by the OFT into complaints of predatory pricing made by the *Daily Telegraph*, *The Guardian* and *The Independent*.

John Bridgeman, Director of Fair Trading, said today: 'I have concluded that News International deliberately made a loss on *The Times* during the period between June 1996 and January 1998 when the Monday edition was sold for 10p, and that this affected competition in the national daily newspaper market. Competitors alleged that they had been forced to cut prices or lose sales and that investment had been reduced accordingly.'

Source: Adapted from an OFT press release

Predatory pricing is an attractive strategy when the market is segmented. For example, a dominant firm can discipline a rival firm in a local market by decreasing its price below costs – without disturbing the prices it charges elsewhere in the market. It is also attractive when the exact cost structure of the dominant firm is not known by its rivals, so that if the firm cuts prices aggressively, the rivals may feel that its cost structure is so low that it can continuously cut prices.

Predatory pricing does not always work, for a number of reasons:

- The rival firms may shut down their capacity and restart once prices have risen. The dominant firm might make excessive losses.

- As one rival firm leaves the market, another may enter after prices rise.

- A victimized firm may be a subsidiary of a larger company who can thus obtain finance from its 'parent' in order to get through a difficult period.

Going-rate pricing

Going-rate pricing is where the firm gives less attention to its own cost structure or demand and more to its competitors' prices.

In oligopolistic industries this feature is often seen in the practice of **parallel pricing** of large petrol dealers such as Shell and Esso, when they charge very similar wholesale prices for petrol within a particular geographic region. The smaller firms in the industry follow the leader and change prices when the market leader changes, rather than when their own demand or costs change.

Such methods are popular when the industry feels that the return is fair and where the elasticity of demand is difficult to measure. It also helps prevent aggressive price wars, although this is not always successful as was evidenced by the 1996 petrol price wars between the oil companies and the supermarkets.

Sealed-bid pricing

Sealed-bid pricing is another form of competitor-based pricing and involves a customer drawing up a detailed specification for a product and putting it out to tender. Each company that wants the contract will then place a bid, and the buyer will, other things being equal, select the supplier which quotes the lowest price.

A major focus for a potential supplier is therefore the likely bid prices of its competitors. Statistical models have been developed to explain this by using the concept of expected profit:

$$\text{Expected profit} = \text{profit} \times \text{probability of winning.}$$

Taking the example of the construction industry where this system is often observed, an individual construction company such as Balfour Beatty, Tarmac, Costain or Wimpey would, on past experience, construct a range of bid prices that might be acceptable to the customer – and would then work out the profit at each bid price together with the probability of that bid being accepted.

As the bid price and profits rise, the probability of the quotation being accepted would, of course, fall. At each bid price, the **expected profit** can then be calculated by using the above equation, and the highest expected profit chosen. The bid price at which the expected profit is highest will then be the bid put to the customer.

Such a system may be suitable for a company which makes many bids since, by learning to play the odds, its long-term profits may be high. However, for companies who bid occasionally or who need contracts badly, this system may not be appropriate.

The system also depends on the availability of efficient competitor information. One Scandinavian ball-bearing manufacturer installed a system which was dependent on its sales force feeding data into a computer on all past successful and unsuccessful bids, in order to build up a data-bank to help it in its future bids.

Market-orientated pricing

This pricing system takes a wider range of factors into consideration when deciding on price. Here we will look at only three of them for illustrative purposes – price skimming, penetration pricing and product line pricing.

Price skimming

Firms often adopt a strategy of **price skimming** when they have a new or special product or service which has few competitors. They charge a high or 'premium' price to a targeted group of customers and 'skim' off the extra profits, before reducing the price to capture a new group of customers.

Companies such as IBM, Polaroid and Bosch have operated such pricing systems. The latter used a successful skimming policy, supported by patents, in its launch of fuel injection and antilock braking systems.

Bombs away in wash war

FELICITY LAWRENCE

A new battle in the 'washing war' between Ariel and Persil loomed yesterday when it emerged the two brands are to launch rival versions of a laundry product – the detergent bomb.

Unilever announced that it would be launching Persil liquid soap capsules at the end of April – only to be outflanked by rival Proctor & Gamble which is said to be ready to send out its new Ariel Liqui-Tabs to shops next month ... The capsules are sachets of pre-measured doses of liquid detergent which can be put in the machine and dissolve on contact with water, thus saving the house spouse the bother of working out how much soap to use ...

As a 'premium-priced product' liquid capsules 'offer good profit opportunities,' Proctor & Gamble told trade customers.

Unilever and Proctor & Gamble are both hoping that liquid capsules will give them an edge, and whoever is first with the innovation is likely to gain a significant advantage

The Guardian, 16 February 2001

Penetration pricing

Some companies may decide to launch products which combine low prices with heavy promotional expenditure, in order to gain a major market share.

This rapid **penetration-pricing** strategy was successfully achieved by the British Motor Corporation (BMC) between 1959 and 1979 when it sold 4.5 million units of its Mini car. The company kept the price of the Mini at the equivalent of less than £500 (based on 1959 prices) over the whole period. Similarly Sony, the Japanese electronics company, temporarily priced its products in the European market at less than the cost of production in order to obtain a market presence.

Obviously, price skimming is more appropriate in market segments where the product provides a high value, where customers have a high ability to pay, where there is a lack of competition, and where there is a high pressure to buy. Conditions for charging low, penetration-based pricing would be where the strategy is to gain rapid market domination or where the aim is to bring down costs by extending demand.

Product-line pricing

Market-orientated companies also have to decide how to price individual products within an existing product line. This is **product-line pricing**.

For example, when Ford developed the Orion motor vehicle it had to carefully price-position the model within its existing product line of Fiesta, Escort, Sierra and Granada.

Similarly, in 2001, Sony had seven digital camcorders in its PC and TRV ranges varying from 440 to 590 grammes in weight and having different combinations of Carl Zeiss lenses, LDC screen sizes, low lux light and horizontal resolution etc. It had to price the cameras according to the difference in costs and prices charged by competitors. For example Sony's PC5 competed with Panasonic's NVMX5 at the £1000 level.

By producing a range of models at different prices, companies hope to cover the different price sensitivities (elasticities of demand) of customers and encourage them to trade-up to the more expensive, higher-margin models.

KEY WORDS

Marketing mix
Cost-plus pricing
Full-cost pricing
Direct-cost pricing
Target-return pricing
Limit pricing
Predatory pricing

Going-rate pricing
Parallel pricing
Sealed-bid pricing
Expected profit
Price skimming
Penetration pricing
Product-line pricing

Further reading

Atkinson, B., Livesey, F. and Milward, R. (eds), Chapter 1 in *Applied Economics*, Macmillan, 1998.

Davies, B. *et al.*, Chapters 2.4 and 3.15 in *Investigating Economics*, Macmillan, 1996.

Griffiths, A. and Wall, S., Chapter 9 in *Applied Economics*, 9th edn, Financial Times/Prentice Hall, 2001.

Hornby, W., Gammie, B. and Wall, S., Chapter 8 in *Business Economics*, 2nd edn, Financial Times/Prentice Hall, 2001.

Useful websites

European Commission: www.europa.eu.int/comm/dgs/competition
Harvard Business Review: www.hbsp.harvard.edu/hbsp/search
Marketing Week: www.marketing-week.co.uk
Office of Fair Trading: www.oft.gov.uk

Essay topics

1. (a) Explain what is meant by each of the following: price discrimination; non-price competition; marginal-cost pricing; limit pricing. [40 marks]

   (b) Evaluate the economic implications of *one* of these pricing strategies from the point of view of both firms and consumers. [60 marks]

   [Edexcel, June 1998]

2. (a) Explain how a monopolist maximizes its profits in the long run. [10 marks]

   (b) Discuss the extent to which profit maximization is a realistic managerial objective for firms. [15 marks]

   [OCR, June 1997]

Data response question

This task is based on a question set by OCR in June 2000. Read the piece below, which covers several aspects of bus services in a fictitious British town. Then, using your knowledge of economics, answer the questions that follow.

Local bus companies set to merge

Covingham, a city situated in the Midlands of England, is currently served by two competing bus companies. Both of the companies have recently been struggling to make a profit. News has recently broken that the two companies plan to merge to become a monopoly supplier of bus services in the city. The news has sparked considerable reaction locally, notably in the letters column of the city's main newspaper. Three recent contributions to the debate have been the following.

- *Extract A: Letter written to the newspaper by the Covingham Association of Bus Users*

In this letter, bus users have expressed their strong concerns about the possible effects on services of a lack of competition between bus companies. An extract from this letter is set out below.

'We are particularly concerned that if the two bus companies merge to form a monopoly in Covingham, then bus fares are likely to rise and that we, the consumers, will have no alternative but to pay those prices or to cease using buses. Furthermore, we consider it to be highly likely that we will begin to see a decline in the standard of the service that is offered to bus users if there is a monopoly and that buses are likely to run less frequently than now when we have two competing operators …'

- *Extract B: Press release by one of the current bus companies*

As one of the current bus operators in Covingham, we are keen to put bus passengers' minds at rest over the proposed merger of the current two companies. There are several significant benefits that we believe will follow this merger:

- There will be a better bus service with more sensibly organized bus times.

- The quality of the bus services will increase as the new larger company will be able to afford to put more investment into the company.
- There will be lower costs per passenger as we will be able to spread fixed costs, such as managerial costs, over a larger number of passengers.
- Our costs will be further lowered owing to a range of economies of scale that will be available to the new larger company.
- We shall be able to finance a campaign to get people back onto buses in Covingham.

All of these developments should be of potential benefit to the bus users of Covingham, and thus we are pleased to recommend the proposed merger to them.

- *Extract C: Research by a student at Covingham University*

A student of Economics at Covingham University is currently investigating the possible economic effects of the proposed merger upon the bus market in Covingham. She has recently conducted some studies on the local bus market to provide relevant data for this work. Two particular pieces of information that she sees as significant are as follows.

Calculations made of the changes in demand for a typical bus journey as the price of the bus journey changes:

Price	Peak demand (journeys per day)	Off-peak demand (journeys per day)
30p	1 100	900
40p	1 050	700
50p	1 000	500
60p	950	300
70p	900	100

There appear to be significant 'positive externalities' to the city if more people travel by bus. She believes these include reduced travel times owing to less road congestion, and cleaner air owing to reduced pollution.

1. (a) Explain the difference between fixed and variable costs.
   [2 marks]
   (b) To what extent can the marginal costs of a bus company be considered fixed costs? [3 marks]
   (c) Identify and explain *two* possible economies of scale that could arise from the proposed merger. [4 marks]
2. (a) Define price elasticity of demand. [2 marks]
   (b) Calculate the price elasticity of demand if the price for a typical off-peak journey rises from its current 50p to 60p. Explain what this figure means. [4 marks]
   (c) If the two bus companies were to merge, discuss the possible scope for price discrimination in the local bus market. [5 marks]
3. (a) Using a diagram, explain the concept of 'positive externalities' as mentioned in extract C. [6 marks]
   (b) Explain what information the Economics student might have required to calculate the benefits arising from bus travel and the problems involved in such calculations. [8 marks]
4. (a) State *two* characteristics of a monopoly market. [2 marks]
   (b) Using a diagram, explain how a monopoly would set its price if it were aiming to maximize its profit. [4 marks]
   (c) Bus users in Covingham have stated their concerns about higher fares and a lower quality of service if the merger goes ahead. Discuss the extent to which these concerns might be justified. [10 marks]

Chapter Nine

Competition and regulation

'People of the same trade seldom meet together, even for merriment and diversion, but when they do the conversation ends in a conspiracy against the public, or in some contrivance to raise price.'
Adam Smith

COMPETITION POLICY

Competition policy is the term applied to various measures used by governments to regulate the environment in which businesses operate. The aim of such measures is to create a more competitive environment by minimizing the economic distortions that occur in the marketplace which often result in lower levels of welfare for both consumers and producers alike.

Economic distortions can occur when, for example, a company with a strong market position abuses that position, or when a few influential firms form a cartel to control the supply of a particular good in a given market.

Although the aim of competition policy is to minimize the negative effects of such distortions, the rationale for such intervention by the state depends on one's view of market structures.

Approaches to competition

The traditional textbook approach

In the **traditional textbook approach,** the term 'competition' is equated with the market structure known as 'perfect competition' (see Chapter 3). The perfect market assumes the existence of a large number of firms each producing identical products; that entry and exit into and out of the industry is completely free; and that each firm has no market power at all. As a result, each firm produces output up to the level where price is equal to marginal cost so that resources have been allocated optimally.

On the other hand, the textbook theory of monopoly presents an industry dominated by one firm, where there is generally no possibility of entry to the industry. In this case, price is above marginal cost so that resources are not allocated optimally.

When one compares these two models, then the textbook case against the abuse of power by the monopolist becomes quite powerful – as you saw in Chapter 4. Hence there are strong reasons in theory why governments need to introduce an effective competition policy.

The workable competition approach

The aim of the **workable competition approach** is to get away from the simple, and often unrealistic theoretical model building. For example, this approach argues that the concept of perfect competition, with its requirement of a large number of firms each producing identical products, is too unrealistic in a complex and dynamic world.

The workable competition approach stresses that an industry should be judged in terms of how it *performs*, and not just in terms, say, of the number of firms in that industry. The aim of the workable competition approach is to try to define what a 'good' performance means in terms of price/cost/welfare and then find the type of industrial structure which provides that level of performance.

The aim of government competition policy in this situation would be to take each industry on a case-by-case basis and try to direct the industry towards the structure that will provide this 'good' performance.

The Austrian approach

The **Austrian approach** assumes that any form of competition must be placed in its dynamic context. In other words, firms continually develop new techniques of production and new products over time in waves of 'creative destruction' as old products/processes die and new ones emerge. Such markets are often dominated by entrepreneurs who are constantly trying to become 'temporary monopolists' as they attempt to break down existing monopolies and enter markets which offer high profits.

This approach is derived from the work of the Austrian economist Friedrich Von Hayek and others. They stressed that the old textbook theories were too static and that monopoly power, for example, should not always be viewed in a negative light. They argued that monopolies may use their profits for essential innovative research and that there is no need to worry about such companies, since these profits will be eroded *over time* by new and more dynamic companies entering the industry.

This view of the competitive process seems to imply that there is less need for government competition policy because the dynamism of the market will solve these dilemmas over time.

Advantages and disadvantages of competition policy

We have seen that the relevance of competition policy depends very much on which approach is taken. The standard textbook approach tends to stand at odds with the Austrian approach, while the workable competition approach appears to lie somewhere between the two extremes. It is no surprise, therefore, that argument about the pros and cons of government competition policy depends on one's view of the competitive process.

At this stage it might be beneficial to discuss briefly the arguments for and against the use of competition policy as a means of increasing efficiency and welfare.

Arguments in favour of competition-based polices

- *Price levels.* It is argued that government policies geared to increasing competition might help to keep prices at the perfectly competitive level, where price would be equated to marginal costs in the long run with firms making normal profits. On the other hand a monopoly, or other form of imperfect structure, would be expected to charge a higher price – at a point where marginal cost equals marginal revenue.

- *Output levels.* Competition policy ensures that output is higher than in imperfect or regulated markets, as seen above.

- *Efficiency levels.* Under competitive conditions, firms are said to be operating at a point where price equals marginal cost and where average costs are at their minimum in the long run – as explained in Chapter 3. A competition policy based on such ideas would result in a more allocatively efficient level of output.

- *Consumer welfare levels.* Competition policy can help prevent the loss of consumer welfare which often results from monopoly and other imperfect markets.

- *Profit levels.* Competition policy helps to prevent excessive or supernormal profits being earned by monopolies or cartels, which often keep prices at abnormally high levels.

- *Entry and exit levels.* Competition policy will help lower entry and exit levels, thus helping to prevent incumbent firms from dominating the industry.

Arguments against competition-based policies

- *Price levels.* Prices may already be lower under imperfect conditions – for example, a monopoly may reap economies of scale and scope which will bring prices below the perfectly competitive level.

- *Output levels.* Given economies of scale and scope, large dominant firms can produce a higher output than under perfectly competitive conditions.

- *Efficiency levels.* Some dominant firms or those who engage in collaborative activities often engage in dynamic activities. For example, those who pool their R&D resources may create cheaper and more innovative projects and bring them to market more quickly.

- *Consumer welfare levels.* The loss of some consumer welfare as a result of a firm dominating a market has to be weighed against producer welfare benefits and the gains to shareholders if profits are above normal for the industry.

- *Profit levels.* Part of the supernormal profits earned by firms may be used to invest in risky but essential innovative research which banks may not be willing to fund.

- *Entry and exit levels.* Exploitation is often short-lived because dynamic changes in the market take away the original reasons for a monopoly or restrictive practice.

Competition policy in the UK

The Competition Act 1998

The **Competition Act** (outlined in the box) is administered by the **Office of Fair Trading** (OFT) and is applied and enforced by the Director General of Fair Trading (DGFT). Investigations into the unfair practices and also appeals against the decisions taken by the Director General are heard by the Competition Commission.

In relation to 'Chapter 1 prohibitions', the DGFT takes the view that an agreement will generally have no appreciable effect on competition if the parties' combined share of the relevant market does not exceed 25 per cent, although this might not be the case in all situations. For example, an agreement which fixes prices, imposes minimum resale prices, or shares markets may be affecting competition even though the market share falls below 25 per cent.

In the case of 'Chapter 2 prohibitions', there is no set market share for defining dominance – although the DGFT considers it unlikely that an undertaking will be dominant if its market share is below 40 per cent either in a specific product market or a specific geographical market under consideration. To determine whether dominance can be proven, the type and nature of entry barriers have to be investigated. The second test is whether a firm has *actually* abused its dominant position. Here, the Competition Act provides a number of criteria for testing whether prices are excessive or price discrimination is being practised. The maximum financial penalty for those found guilty can be up to 10 per cent of their turnover.

The Competition Act

In the UK, the main regulations covering the nature of competition are laid down in the Competition Act of 1998. The Act seeks to promote a competitive environment by prohibiting certain agreements which seek to prevent fair competition from taking place. The two main areas of prohibitions in the act are as follows.

Chapter 1 prohibitions prohibit agreements which prevent, restrict or distort competition within the UK. They include agreements between companies to fix selling prices; agreements to share markets; agreements to regulate the terms and conditions on which goods or services are to be supplied; and agreements to share sensitive and confidential information, such as sharing price information amongst a few operators.

Chapter 2 prohibitions prohibit large undertakings from abusing their dominant position in the marketplace. Such abusive conduct generally involves charging excessively high prices; engaging in price discrimination; predatory pricing; refusing to supply existing or potential competitors; and arrangements between suppliers and purchasers which restrict the commercial freedom of one or more party (vertical restraints). An example of the latter would be when a main manufacturer supplies only a limited number of retailers provided they meet a certain standard of service etc.

The Fair Trading Act 1973

The **Fair Trading Act** covers much of the present UK legislation regarding monopolies, mergers and acquisitions. The DGFT can make a reference to the Competition Commission in order to establish whether a scale monopoly situation exists – that is, where a single company or group of companies supplies or acquires at least 25 per cent of the goods and services of a particular type in all, or part, of the UK.

Similarly, a complex monopoly occurs when a group of companies which are not connected, but which account for at least 25 per cent of the market, have engaged in conduct which is likely to have the effect of restricting or distorting competition.

As far as mergers and acquisitions are concerned, the Act stipulates that in order to qualify for investigation the merger must result in a situation where the merged firms would control 25 per cent or more of the relevant market, or must involve gross worldwide assets exceeding £70 million.

In both monopolies and mergers, the DGFT advises the Secretary of State for Trade and Industry as to which cases to refer to the Competition Commission for investigation.

The EU experience

The European countries have long histories of state intervention in markets, so it is not surprising that the European Commission accepts the case for intervention by member governments.

Apart from agriculture, competition is the only area for which the EU has been able to effectively implement a common policy across member states. The Commission can intervene to control the behaviour of monopolists and to increase the degree of competition through authority derived directly from the Treaty of Rome. The relevant articles controlling competition are outlined below.

- **Article 81** prohibits agreements between enterprises that result in restrictions of competition which may affect trade between member states. It is the basis of the 'Chapter 1 prohibitions' in the UK Competition Act.

- **Article 82** prohibits a dominant firm or group of firms from using their market power to exploit consumers which may affect trade between member states. It is the basis of the 'Chapter 2 prohibitions' of the UK system.

- **Articles 87 and 88** prohibit government subsidies to industries or individual firms which distort, or threaten to distort, competition across the EU.

Competition policy in action in the UK

Cartel theory

A **cartel** is a collusive agreement among sellers to limit competition by fixing prices/output or by other measures, in order to gain higher profits.

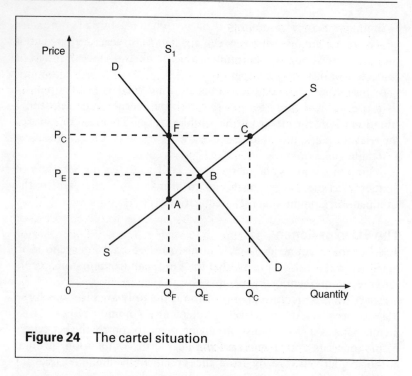

Figure 24 The cartel situation

An example of a cartel situation is given in Figure 24. In a competitive market, the equilibrium price would be at P_E with output Q_E. However, if the market were transformed into a cartel by firms limiting total output to Q_F, then the supply curve would become kinked (SAFS$_1$) instead of being the normal supply curve SS. As a result, price would rise to P_C. This cartel will continue to be successful provided that:

- the elasticity of demand is relatively low
- the elasticity of supply is also low
- there is no tendency for members of the cartel to cheat
- barriers to entry are high.

If enough members of the cartel are tempted to cheat, or if new firms can enter the industry easily, then supply will increase from F towards C. As a result, a surplus equal to FC would appear on the market at price P_C, creating pressure for the price to fall back towards P_E as the cartel breaks down.

Price-fixing cartel: discounts
In February 2000, the OFT revealed the details of a secret price-fixing cartel that had been in operation between 1994 and 1996. It involved 12 Volvo dealers operating in Hertfordshire, West Sussex, London, Berkshire, Kent, Hampshire and Surrey. The agreement between the dealers restricted discount rates available to commercial and retail customers to 2.5 per cent for the basic ranges, while no discount was offered on certain prestige ranges. Such an agreement tended to limit any price competition between the dealers.

Price-fixing cartel: information exchange
In December 1999, the OFT discovered that Vitafoam Ltd of Rochdale, Carpenter plc of Glossop, Derbyshire, and Recticel Ltd of Alferton, Derbyshire, had met to agree on price rises of 8 per cent for foam rubber and 4 per cent for reconstituted foam which they supplied to the upholstery business. Cartel members agreed that the price rises announced by Vitafoam, the market leader, would be matched immediately by similar announcements from Carpenter and Recticel.

Price-fixing cartels: resale pricing
In August 2000, Waterline Ltd – a company that bought electrical goods from manufacturers and then sold them on to other companies to install in kitchens etc. – had published a recommended resale price (RRP) list for certain electrical goods. Waterline had suggested to its customers, the kitchen fitting companies, that they should adhere to the recommended prices. However this was found to be against the public interest as it prevented any discounting by the kitchen companies which would have benefited the general public.

Similarly, in August 1999 the OFT obtained assurances from the kit manufacturers Gilbert and Pollard Sports Ltd, Puma UK and Asics (UK) Ltd that they would not try to enforce minimum resale prices on their products; that is, they would not prevent retailers from charging less than their recommended list prices for replica football kits.

Supply-fixing cartel
The three largest UK producers of ordinary Portland cement (OPC) – Blue Circle plc, Castle Cement Ltd and the Rugby Group –refused to supply bulk OPC to customers such as readymix concrete producers who had intended to resell it in bags to builders' merchants. This was because they themselves sold OPC in bag form to customers. In September 2000, the companies agreed to supply cement for resale

after the OFT found that refusing to supply OPC in bulk for ultimate resale in bags was anti-competitive.

Competition policy in practice in the EU

Anti-competitive practices

In September 2000, the European Commission – under Article 81 – imposed a fine of 43 billion euros on Opel Nederland BV, the Dutch importer of cars of the Opel brand, and its parent company General Motors Nederland BV. The fine was imposed for preventing car dealers in the Netherlands from selling new Opel cars to non-Netherlands customers at the relatively cheap prices existing in the Netherlands. The Commission felt that Opel dealers in the Netherlands were being prevented from exploiting competition advantages as a result of the price differences in EU markets. It was felt that this acted against one of the most fundamental objectives of the Single Market.

Abuses of dominant position

In March 2000, the European Commission declared the proposed acquisition by Volvo (the Swedish truck producer) of Scania (another Swedish truck manufacturer) to be incompatible with the common market. This horizontal merger would have created a dominant position for the company in that it would have controlled 31 per cent of all market sales in the European Economic Area (EEA). In particular, the acquisition would have created a dominant position in the heavy trucks market of Sweden, Norway, Finland and Ireland, as well as in the market for touring coaches in Finland and the UK.

The Commission also concluded that the entry barriers into the sector were high since it would have taken a huge investment to challenge the Volvo/Scania deal.

In December 2000, the Commission re-adopted three further decisions fining the Belgium company Solvay and the British company ICI, for abusing their dominant position in the soda ash market in the 1980s. They had developed a two-tier pricing system where they sold a basic or 'core' tonnage at the normal price to customers but any additional quantities they offered at a substantial secret discount in order to keep out any potential second supplier. Although this was a serious infringement of Article 82, the Court of Justice saw fit to annul the fines on proceedural grounds. Now, the Commission with its 'long memory', has re-adopted the decisions in their proper form and fined Solvay and ICI – 23 million and 10 million euros respectively.

PRIVATIZATION AND REGULATION POLICY

The first part of this chapter discussed how the UK and the EU have tried to increase industrial efficiency by controlling the potential abusive power of monopolies and cartels in the private sector.

In this part of the chapter we will investigate three key areas:

- how the UK government has tried to increase industrial efficiency by transferring its industrial assets to the private sector (**privatization**)

- how the government sets out to control large privatized utilities, which often are 'natural monopolies', from abusing their power (**agency regulation**)

- the nature of deregulation in the private sector.

Privatization

Advantages of privatization

There are many reasons why the UK government has privatized the state's industrial assets over the last twenty years or so.

- *To improve economic efficiency.* The privatized enterprise is exposed to increased economic competition from other private sector competitors, so helping to enhance its efficiency.

- *To widen share ownership.* The availability of new shares on the market creates a new group of shareholders – workers and managers. This can help to develop an 'enterprise culture'.

- *To reduce government debt.* The sale of state-owned enterprises means that the government no longer needs to borrow money to finance these enterprises, thus decreasing the public sector net cash requirement – i.e. decreasing government debt obligations.

- *To change managerial control.* The privatization movement should result in fewer administrative problems for government, and might decrease potential union conflicts given that the nationalized industries often had militant unions.

Criticisms of privatization

Critics of privatization have pointed out that there are dangers in allowing the private sector to control such important industries.

- *Public sector efficiency.* It is argued that technological innovations would have occurred in these industries even if they continued to be owned by the state. Consumers might prefer a publicly owned industry because privatization can lead to excess profits, which are used to benefit shareholders and executives rather than consumers.

- *Undervaluation of state assets.* This argument points to the fact that state assets are sometimes sold at too low a price, in order to speed up the privatization process. This is a waste of valuable resources. Also, it means that taxpayers, who were effectively the owners of nationalized industries, are paying for them twice over when they buy shares in the newly privatized concerns.

- *Concentration of share ownership.* Far from helping to *widen* shareholdership, the privatization process can lead people to buy the shares and then sell them for a windfall profit. These shares are bought by financial institutions, thus leading to a fall in the percentage of shares held by private investors.This can lead to a *concentration* of shareownership in the hands of financial institutions rather than creating a 'shareholding democracy'.

- *Short termism.* It is argued that although selling state assets can reduce the government's net cash requirements (i.e. its borrowing) – this can only have a 'one off' effect on the finances and does not solve future government debt problems. Also, the tendency for the private sector to want quick returns on investment may turn out to be inappropriate for the utilities sector where investment is in long-term assets and the payback period tends to be lengthy.

Regulation of utilities

The privatization of utilities such as telephone, gas and water during the 1980s and 1990s created a danger that these bodies would merely change from being government-controlled monopolies to being private monopolies that would exploit consumers. To avoid such potential exploitation, the government had to introduce control mechanisms to regulate the privatized utilities.

Various **regulatory agencies** were set up to make sure that these utilities would operate in the most effective way to stimulate efficient production and consumer benefits. For example, agencies were set up for telecommunications (OFTEL), gas and electricity supply (OFGEM), water (OFWAT), railways (ORR), and electricity/gas in Northern Ireland (OFREG).

Each sector has a regulator whose duty it is:

- *to stimulate the effects of a competitive market by setting price caps and performance standards for the companies in that sector.* For example, regulators lay down a maximum allowable price increase, decided by a *capping formula.* The increase is limited to the percentage rise in the retail price index (RPI) minus and/or plus certain other specified percentages.

In the case of the telecommunications industry, its regulator OFTEL controls the price of such things as connection charges, residential line rental and. direct dialled calls. In 2001 it used the formula RPI-X, where X reflects the cost reductions and efficiency savings which the regulator expects the telecommunications companies to make during the price control period. It is expected that these cost reductions are passed on the consumer, so that companies such as BT, Mercury and cable operators are only allowed to increase prices by the *difference* between the resale price index (RPI) and this X value (4.5% in 2001). For example if the RPI was 5.5% during the control period, then the regulator would allow the companies to increases their prices by only 5.5%- 4.5% = 1%. OFGEM uses.a similar formula to control the prices of the fourteen Public Electricity Companies (PES) which distribute electricity.

In the case of OFWAT, the formula for 2001 was RPI- K - where K represented a number of variables such as past performance of water companies, expected efficiency gains, water quality improvements, enhanced security of supplies, and service levels etc. The nature of variables such as X and K are determined by the regulator in consultation with the utility companies and the content (and absolute percentage value) of these variables are changed from time to time. In this way, regulators can control prices to prevent utility companies from abusing their market power and earning abnormal profits.

The regulators' duty is also:

- *to encourage actual competition by making it easier for new producers to enter the industry – in order to prevent the industry being dominated by a monopoly producer.* The case of gas supply is an interesting example of this process. When British Gas was first privatized it had a classical natural monopoly in the supply of gas. However, by the end of 1999 the company's market share had been eroded as a result of competition from other companies (e.g. electricity companies) in the supply of gas to domestic and industrial users.

Problems for regulators

The main benefit from regulating the pricing strategies of privatized utilities is that it eliminates most of the disadvantages of monopoly power, as outlined in Chapter 4. You are advised to re-read the appropriate part of that chapter, with the subject of regulation in mind.

On the other hand, regulating such industries sometimes creates major problems for regulators as they try to control the industry for the benefit of consumers.

Npower in trouble for its selling tactics

In January 2001 OFGEM, the regulator of the gas and electricity industries, criticised npower for its high-pressure sales tactics. The regulators had received a high number of complaints from the general public. Some people claimed they had been misled into signing a supply contract with npower by being told they were completing a survey.

OFGEM gave npower a year to reduce the number of complaints. It was told if it failed to achieve this the regulator would take action. The regulator has the power to stop the company taking on new customers and to improve a fine equivalent to 10 per cent of the company's turnover.

- *Consumer interests versus producer interests.* The control of prices when the demand for the services of the utility is inelastic will prevent the regulated industry from raising prices and therefore its revenue. While this policy may benefit consumers, it leads to a fall in shareholder profits and share prices, and reduced future investment in the industry.

- *Pricing caps.* The setting of a price cap for the utilities may result in low returns and job losses in those industries. Therefore, lower prices for consumers may lead to unemployment and increased cost to government in the form of unemployment and other welfare payments.

- *Structural changes.* Utilities, such as electricity, were split up during privatization so that the generating sector and the distribution sector were not present in one big organization. Nevertheless, a wave of large vertical takeovers occurred in the mid-1990s which have brought back into existence large monopoly-type organizations in the utilities.

- *Organization and costs of regulation.* It may be excessively costly to run many regulatory agencies, and can lead to inconsistencies in approaches to competition policy across different sectors. Concentration of all regulation in one agency might be more efficient and lead to more consistent treatment.

Deregulation

The term 'regulation' may be defined as the various rules *set out* by government or their agencies that seek to control the operations of firms for the benefit of the public. The word is often used in relation to the control of previously owned government organizations that now have monopoly-type power in certain markets (e.g. utilities), as you saw in the previous section.

However, the word 'regulation' is also used to cover a wider range of controls which have been imposed by government in other areas of activity. An example is the Road Traffic Acts which regulate bus traffic by controlling the issuing of operators' licences, the quality of vehicles, the level of fares etc.

On the other hand, the term **deregulation** refers to efforts by government to remove various rules that seek to control the operations of firms. In other words, it involves the question of whether, and to what extent, government regulation should be replaced by market forces.

Deregulation therefore covers both the privatization process and the wider relaxing of controls on other sectors such as the bus industry as noted above. We have already discussed the deregulation (i.e. privatization) of nationalized industries, so to end this chapter we look briefly at the pros and cons of the deregulation process in the private sector bus industry, as seen in Table 13.

This industry was regulated by the Road Traffic Act of 1930 and was deregulated by the 1985 Transport Act. Argument still continues as to whether this is the best long-run strategy for the industry, and Table 13 provides an example of the pros and cons of deregulation in the industry.

Table 13 Deregulation in the bus industry

Advantages	Disadvantages
• Increased competition gives greater consumer choice and is more responsive to consumer needs	• Wasteful duplication of services on profitable routes
• Greater potential for new innovations (e.g. mini buses)	• Increase in levels of congestion in some urban areas
• Reduction of government subsidies to bus companies will weed out inefficient operators	• Reduction of subsidies may lead to rise in level of prices and a fall in bus use
• Increased freedom of entry into the industry for new companies	• Larger bus companies may take over others, leading to local monopolies

---

KEY WORDS

Competition policy	Fair Trading Act
Traditional textbook approach	Articles 81, 82, 87, 88
Workable competition	Cartel
approach	Privatization
Austrian approach	Regulatory agencies
Competition Act	Deregulation
Office of Fair Trading	

Further reading

Atkinson, B., Livesey, F. and Milward, R. (eds), Chapters 5 and 6 in *Applied Economics*, Macmillan, 1998.

Bamford, C., Chapter 5 in *Transport Economics*, 3rd edn, Heinemann Educational, 2001.

Office of Fair Trading, *The Competition Act 1998: The Major Provisions*, OFT40, March 1999.

Sloman, J., Chapter 12 in *Economics*, 4th edn, Prentice Hall Europe, 2000.

Useful websites

OECD: Competition law and policy: www.oecd.org/daf/clp/annrep.htm
European Commission: www.europa.eu.int/comm/dgs/competition
Office of Fair Trading: www.oft.gov.uk
Regulators:
    OFGEM: www.ofgem.gov.uk
    OFTEL: www.oftel.gov.uk
    OFWAT: www.ofwat.gov.uk
    ORR: www.rail-reg.gov.uk

Essay topics

1. 'Once a market such as the telecommunications market or the water market becomes sufficiently contestable, regulation is no longer needed.'

    (a) Choosing a utility industry, such as telecommunications or water, explain the factors which may affect the contestability of the market. [20 marks]

    (b) Assess the case for and against abolishing the agency, such as OFTEL or OFWAT, which is currently responsible for regulating the industry. [30 marks]

    [AQA, 2000]

2. (a) Explain how the regulators in the UK have attempted to prevent the privatized utilities from abusing their monopoly power.

[12 marks]

(b) Using examples to support your arguments, assess the strengths and weaknesses of the UK's approach to regulating privatized industries. [13 marks]

[Associated Examining Board, June 1998]

Conclusion

It is hoped that you will have understood and enjoyed this book. It might have helped in the following ways.

- You need to have a clear view of why firms exist and why they grow, diversify and, sometimes, contract over time. Firms do not 'stand still' – and an appreciation of this fact is important for any student of business. This aspect is made more relevant when it is realized that the objective which firms pursue can also vary over time as the business environment changes.

- You need to appreciate that every business organization has to be fully aware of the major cost and revenue factors which affect the decision of how much of a good or service should be produced.

- You need to understand that markets, like people, come in different shapes and sizes. An insight into the conditions necessary for markets to be at their most efficient is needed in order to understand why real-world markets are often imperfect.

- You have to realize that in the business world a single company or a group of companies often attempt to take advantage of their strong position in the market by attempting to control the supply of a good or service – often to the detriment of consumers.

- You need to appreciate that, in a complex world, companies often decide on their own strategy only after trying to take into consideration the possible response of their rivals. Business is often a game of calculated chance.

- You must understand that the degree of profit earned by companies in any market depends on the ease with which other firms can enter or leave that industry.

- You need to appreciate that all firms are concerned about how to determine a price level which will give them sufficient profits while also being attractive to consumers.

Finally, you must recognize that the government has a dynamic role in the business environment. This includes introducing systems to improve market efficiency by preventing companies from abusing their market power to the detriment of consumers, while also helping to provide companies with a business environment where unnecessary regulation is absent.

Index